AA308

Thought and Experience: Themes in the Philosophy of Mind

BOOK 1

Aspects of Mind

SEAN CRAWFORD

This publication forms part of an Open University course AA308 *Thought and Experience: Themes in the Philosophy of Mind*. Details of this and other Open University courses can be obtained from the Course Information and Advice Centre, PO Box 724, The Open University, Milton Keynes MK7 6ZS, United Kingdom: tel. +44 (0)1908 653231, email general-enquiries@open.ac.uk

Alternatively, you may visit the Open University website at http://www.open.ac.uk where you can learn more about the wide range of courses and packs offered at all levels by The Open University.

To purchase a selection of Open University course materials visit the webshop at www.ouw.co.uk, or contact Open University Worldwide, Michael Young Building, Walton Hall, Milton Keynes MK7 6AA, United Kingdom for a brochure. tel. +44 (0) 1908 858785; fax +44 (0)1908 858787; email ouwenq@open.ac.uk

The Open University
Walton Hall, Milton Keynes
MK7 6AA

First published 2005

Edited, designed and typeset by The Open University.

Printed and bound in the United Kingdom by The Bath Press, Bath.

ISBN 0 7492 9641 0

1.1

207230b/aa308b1i1.1

Contents

READINGS

Preface

This book is an introduction to some issues in the philosophy of mind. It examines some contemporary accounts of the nature of mind and mental phenomena as well as considering what some of the philosophers of the ancient and recent past have said about them. The reason for looking at the history of the philosophy of mind is that it has to a great extent determined the way that the philosophy of mind is now pursued and a good understanding of current debates demands at least some familiarity with the historical background.

Many introductions to the philosophy of mind begin with dualism, Descartes's substance dualism in particular. One reason for this appears to be the thought that dualism is the default, commonsense view of the mind and that it is therefore natural to begin by examining it. There may be some truth in this and indeed we will spend a good deal of time examining some of Descartes's views about the mind, his views on sensation in particular. But it is important to appreciate that there is also a sense in which Descartes's substance dualism is very radical, in that it goes against a long standing philosophical and commonsense tradition, according to which only things made of organic matter, only living, biological kinds can have minds – at least that only a living thing could have a mind like ours, with its capacity for consciousness, rational thought, sensation and perception, language, creative imagination and complex emotions and personalities. This view that minded creatures are essentially a subclass of living creatures was deeply rooted in the classical and medieval Aristotelian traditions in philosophy that preceded Descartes, and one of his most profound breaks with this tradition is his rejection of the idea that there is an essential connection between mentality and life. This idea has perhaps been even more influential than his dualism and is at the very core of some current functionalist theories of mind.

The first chapter of the book begins on an ahistorical note, by exploring the wide variety and nature of, as well as the relations among, mental phenomena, and the kinds of thing that we think intuitively seem to have minds of some kind. In Chapter 2, we then turn to the aforementioned key historical development in the philosophy of mind, namely, Descartes's replacement of the Aristotelian notion of the mind as the soul of a living creature with the idea of the mind as an immaterial substance attached in a special way to a bodily machine. We will explore the extremely problematic nature of sensation that Descartes's view gives rise to. Is sensation an aspect of the body or of the mind, according to him? The fate of the animals hangs here in the balance, for whether they can be said to have sensations depends on how he answers this question. In the third chapter we turn to Gilbert Ryle's famous attack on Descartes's concept of mind as the 'ghost in the machine' and examine his account of the mind, in which he attempts to substitute an 'outer' conception of the mental for Descartes's 'inner' conception. Chapter 4 introduces modern materialist and functionalist conceptions of mind and Chapter 5 brings the story relatively up to date by considering the computational theory of mind. No familiarity with the philosophy of mind is presupposed and the book should be accessible to those with little or even no familiarity with philosophy in general but who are willing to read carefully and think hard.

I would like to thank my colleagues Alex Barber, Mike Beaney, Keith Frankish, Carolyn Price and Peter Wright for valuable comments and criticisms on earlier drafts and for providing many helpful suggestions about how to improve the material. Peter Wright's editing, in particular, saved me from many stylistic infelicities as well as pedagogical and philosophical errors. I am also very grateful to Jerry Fodor and Susan James for taking the time to be interviewed on the CD that accompanies this book; and to David Blount for his excellent handling of the production process. My greatest debt, however, is to Mike Beaney, not only for his excellent comments on the written and audio material and his suggestions about the substance and organization of it, but also for many great philosophical conversations we had while driving to work.

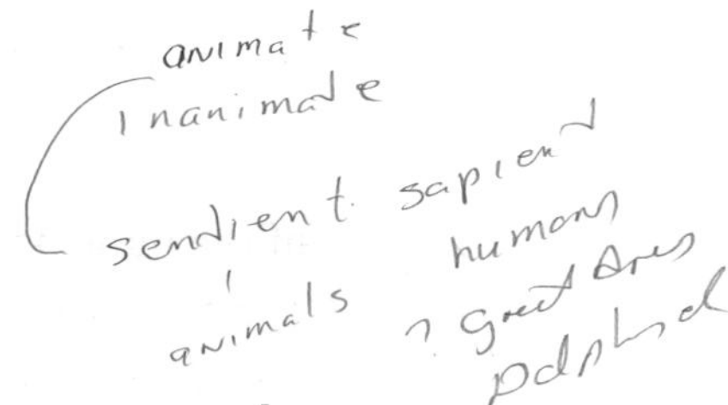

CHAPTER 1

Introduction: Minds and Mental Phenomena

The quick and the dead – the minded and the non-minded

Two of the most fundamental contrasts we draw are between living and non-living things – the animate and inanimate – and between things with minds or mentality and those without. Rocks and chairs are pieces of inanimate matter; they are not just dead, they are the kinds of things that can never have been alive, at least not in their present form. Plants, however, are living organisms, as are animals. But while plants are alive they do not have any kind of mental life. Their activities include nutrition, growth and reproduction, but they are not sentient; they have no sensations or sensory awareness or consciousness of the world around them. Plants do not undergo any experiences; they are not 'awake'. While they certainly exhibit responses to various sorts of stimuli, it would be stretching it to say they perceive things in their environment or that they have inner experiences or sensations, that they can, for example, feel pain. Animals, of course, are sentient beings, or at least many animals are, for they are aware of their environment, in the sense that they can perceive, to varying degrees, what goes in it. Moreover, many animals, though perhaps not all, have inner experiences and sensations; they can feel pain, for example, and experience fear and pleasure – at least it certainly seems that way.

Among the animals, there are those that are not only sentient but also sapient: they have some kind of intellectual capacity for understanding, thinking, reasoning and knowing – in short, they have the capacity for rational thought and action. But just which animals fall into the category of sapience is a vexing question. Certainly human animals are sapient – we dignify our species with the name *Homo sapiens*, after all. But is anything else sapient? What about birds, dogs, apes and dolphins? There seems little doubt that they perceive and feel. But do they have thoughts? Do they really understand, know and reason about things? Philosophers are notoriously divided on the question. Ancient and medieval philosophers, such as Aristotle (384–322 BCE) and St Thomas Aquinas (1225–74), were of the firm opinion that animals lacked the capacity for thought and reason, though they believed that animals certainly had feelings and sensations. The famous French philosopher-scientist René Descartes (1596–1650) concurred that animals are indeed 'thoughtless brutes', entirely without reason – but he went even further, suggesting by implication that they lacked feelings and sensations and indeed consciousness altogether. Animals, on this view, are mere 'automata', entirely devoid of conscious experience. This radical opinion of Descartes provoked his contemporary Henry More (1614–87), the Cambridge Platonist, who agreed with Descartes on many other matters, to write to him in a letter that 'There is none of your opinions that my soul, gentle and tender as it is, shrinks from as much as that murderous and cutthroat view you maintain in the *Discourse*, that deprives the brutes of all life and sense' (quoted by Wilson 1999, 495). As we shall see, it is not quite right to say that Descartes denied life to animals; that he denied them 'sense', however, is virtually beyond debate, and shows that the distinction between animals as sentient and plants as non-sentient has been disputed. We shall examine Descartes's position on this most controversial of opinions in the next chapter; for the moment, let us assume, with commonsense, that More is right against Descartes and note that while Descartes and his ancient and medieval predecessors disagree about whether animals are sentient they all agree that they are not sapient. This by itself may seem enough of an affront to commonsense. Animal lovers, however, may take some comfort in the fact that not all philosophers deny reason to animals. The Scottish philosopher David Hume (1711–76) roundly declared that 'no truth appears to me more evident, than that beasts are endow'd with thought and reason as well as men' and that 'the arguments are in this case so obvious, that they never escape the most stupid and ignorant' (Hume 1978, 176). Evidently, the arguments Hume has in mind may nevertheless escape great geniuses, such as Descartes. Not only did these alleged arguments escape Descartes, but he thought he had other arguments that pointed to the opposite conclusion, that animals lack all reason and thought, though he admitted they fell short of conclusively establishing this: 'I do not think it can be proved that there is [no thought in animals] since the human mind does not reach into their hearts' (Descartes 1985, vol. III, 365). His central argument for the conclusion that it is overwhelmingly likely that animals do not have thought is that language use is the only sure sign of rational thought and no animals other than humans use language. Indeed, many people think that the only known sapient creatures are also the only known language users and that this strongly suggests that only language users are capable of having real thought – despite the anthropomorphizing of some pet owners. On the other side, one may reply that given the truly remarkable things that some languageless creatures are capable of, only absurdly strong or unreasonably stingy notions of belief, thought and knowledge could be used to deny them these capacities. Consider Wolfgang Kohler's (1887–1967) celebrated studies of the mentality of apes (Kohler 1925). He placed bananas out of reach of his chimpanzees but supplied them with boxes and sticks that would enable them to obtain the fruit if used in the right way. The chimps proceeded to stack boxes to climb in order to reach the fruit with the long sticks. It is very hard not to think of the chimps as solving a problem by thinking and planning in some sense. The English philosopher John Locke (1632–1704) expresses a typically cautious view (with a parenthetical remark probably directed at Descartes):

> if they have any ideas at all, and are not bare machines (as some would have them) we cannot deny them to have some reason. It seems as evident to me, that they do some of them in certain instances reason, as that they have sense; but it is only in particular ideas, just as they received them from their senses. They are the best of them tied up within those narrow bounds, and *have not* (as I think) the faculty to enlarge them by any kind of *abstraction*.
>
> (Locke 1975, 160)

An animal may reason about particular things, such as the boxes and bananas in its cage, but it cannot employ the abstract concepts *box* and *banana*. Moreover, those with certain religious beliefs may very well want to point out that admitting non-human animals into the club of thinkers is not perforce to admit that they have *souls*. Only humans have souls. But what is it about us, that mere animals lack, in virtue of which we have souls and they do not? Some might say our possession of free will and moral responsibility. No matter how intelligent the chimpanzee may be, it cannot be said to act freely and morally.

'Soul' and 'mind' undoubtedly have different connotations, as do other terms in the lexical neighbourhood, such as 'psyche', 'subject', 'spirit', 'consciousness', 'ego', 'self', 'agent', 'person', 'cognitive system', and so on. There are important differences between the meanings of these terms and their exact meanings are not very clear. Moreover, their relations to the concepts of life, sentience and sapience are matters of intense debate, as is the relation between life, sentience and sapience themselves. Indeed, each single term, for example 'soul', may mean different things to different people and has meant different things to different ages. The pre-Socratic philosopher Thales thought magnets had souls. It is unlikely that he meant the same by 'soul' as, say, later Christian philosophers. Some of these different meanings will be discussed later. For now, let us set aside these issues and assume that there is sufficient overlap between the various terms, as well as a certain degree of univocality among the uses of each term, and provisionally designate this overlap and univocality 'mind' or 'mentality'. In the rest of this chapter, we shall consider, in a preliminary fashion, the kinds of things that might have minds, the various kinds of mental phenomena that exist, and the relation among these various mental phenomena. In the next chapter, we shall return to the issue of (non-human) animal minds when we discuss Descartes's views on animal sensation.

Kinds of minds

Let us then start on the questions of what kinds of things possess or could possess mentality, while remembering that the meaning of the term is somewhat elastic and imprecise.

ACTIVITY

What kind of possible things, other than humans and other animals, might have minds or possess some form of mentality? In each case, briefly state the qualities of the thing in question that make it a possible candidate for a creature with a mind.

DISCUSSION

Three categories of things come readily to my mind: (i) machines, especially electronic machines such as computers and robots; (ii) angels and other spiritual beings; and (iii) extraterrestrial life forms. The reason why one might think that computers might have minds is that computers can calculate and calculation can be a sign of intelligence. Indeed, the English philosopher Thomas Hobbes (1588–1679) claimed that thinking was a kind of calculating when he defined reason as 'nothing but *reckoning*' (1996, 28). The reason why one might think robots have minds is that robots can perform certain seemingly intelligent tasks involving a significant amount of movement on their part and this movement originates from inside them and can be adjusted in accordance with information gleaned from the environment. Angels and spiritual beings have minds because they are conscious and can think. An extraterrestrial life form might be thought to have a mind for any of the reasons already given for machines and spiritual beings, depending on the kind of life form envisaged; it might also be said to have a mind because (possibly unlike spiritual beings) it has sense perception and feelings, and possibly emotions and even a personality.

At the outset we proceeded as if creatures with mentality were a sub-category of living creatures – Aristotle certainly thought this – and mentioned both human and non-human animals as examples. However, in answering the above question, you might have wondered whether it is possible for a machine to have a mind or some kind of mentality. If so, you are in good company, for some cognitive scientists are willing to ascribe beliefs to such lowly machines as thermostats! The philosopher John Searle reports John McCarthy, one of the founders of the field of 'artificial intelligence', as saying that 'machines as simple as thermostats can be said to have beliefs'. Searle asked McCarthy what beliefs his thermostats had, and McCarthy answered: 'My thermostat has three beliefs. My thermostat believes – it's too hot in here, it's too cold in here and it's just right in here (Searle 1984, 30). This probably seems preposterous, an extreme and egregious case of anthropomorphizing which is hard to take seriously. But what about more complex machines, such as computers and robots? Not just today's computers and robots, but also tomorrow's. One line of thought infused in popular culture is the idea that while a robot or computer, built entirely out of non-organic parts, could engage in much of the kind of thinking and reasoning we engage in – indeed, it might even be superior to us in this regard – it could never have a full-blown conscious mental life like ours. It might even be able to have limited visual, auditory and tactile perceptual capacities, in the sense of being able to discriminate accurately among various colours, shapes, sounds and surfaces. But surely no machine could ever experience pain, for example, by touching a burning hot surface, even though it might be able to detect bodily damage to itself caused by touching a hot surface. Moreover, no mere machine could feel emotions like love or jealousy or embarrassment. And even when it comes to perceiving, we are tempted toward scepticism about whether a machine that could detect the presence of coffee or chocolate would really be having any accompanying olfactory and gustatory experiences. Indeed, the plots of some science-fiction stories revolve around certain robots and computers, which are superior to humans in certain cognitive tasks, lacking the full range of human experiences. The robot or android Data in the television series *Star Trek: The Next Generation* is an example. As viewers well know, various comic moments are created by Data's superior intelligence and rationality but absence of emotions. Moreover, it is often said that even the most complex machine is in principle incapable of imagination and creativity: a computer, for example, could never invent anything or produce a work of art. It is not entirely clear why this should be so, but one thought appears to be that machines are governed by strict deterministic principles and creativity and imagination involve the free play of the mind unrestrained by any algorithmic bounds. But how do we know that our minds do not run according to strict deterministic principles?

Another line of thought present in popular culture is that, one day, computers may even be able to have experiences, emotions and creativity. The evil super-computer HAL 9000, for example, in Stanley Kubrick's film *2001: A Space Odyssey* famously exhibits emotions when he is being 'shut down' after murdering some of the human crew of a spaceship. The android Data learns to play the violin and paint. The robot C3PO in the *Star Wars* films exhibits emotions like fear, worry and frustration; though it is not clear whether he is capable of feeling physical pain. The robots or 'replicants' in Ridley Scott's film *Blade Runner* can feel pain and start to develop emotions after building up a bank of life experiences – with disastrous results. Interestingly, however, these 'replicants' are made out of organic materials, they are biological robots, and are only distinguishable from humans by sophisticated tests. Nevertheless, it is clear that even according to this line of thought, there is supposed to be something more amazing or surprising about an emotional or creative robot than there is about a pure thinking or calculating robot. This is no doubt owed partly to the fact that we already have computers that can perform astonishing feats of calculation – witness the fact that the computer Deep Blue has beaten the world chess champion Gary Kasparov – but there is no mechanical device that exhibits even a modicum of the affective side of mental life.

Machines are not the only kinds of non-living, non-organic creatures that are often said to have minds. According to the Christian religion, angels exist and have minds of some kind, as does God, if He exists. What is the mind of an angelic being like? It depends, first of all, on whether angelic beings have material bodies, for we need to know whether they have any sense organs. Opinions about this differ in much the same way as opinions about the nature of the soul differ. Consider, for a moment, the different views about the nature of the soul. Sometimes the soul is thought of as a particularly fine or rarefied material substance with a vaguely humanoid shape. Thus, in the *Iliad* the souls of the dead Homeric heroes are their 'life forces' and are associated with their breath. The souls leave their dead bodies when they heave their last breath and descend to Hades to live out a bleak and shadowy existence. At one point in the *Odyssey*, Odysseus descends to Hades to consult the ghost of the blind prophet Tiresias, with whom he speaks for some time. There is also a tendency to think of souls as completely immaterial substances, with no shape, mass, volume or spatial dimensions at all; not the kinds of things that can be seen or sensed in any way, let alone conversed with, except perhaps under very special circumstances. Returning to angels, St Augustine (354–430) claimed that we do not know whether they have material bodies, and Descartes, at least at one point, thought that 'it is not clear by natural reason alone whether angels are created in the form of minds distinct from matter, or in the form of minds united to matter' (Descartes 1985, vol. III, 380). According to Aquinas and Roman Catholic doctrine, however, angels are purely spiritual beings with no material bodies. But as the literary critic Harold Bloom (1997) points out, in *Paradise Lost* Milton portrays the angels as embodied beings eating human food. And anyone who has seen western religious art (such as romanesque mosaics, gothic icons and Renaissance paintings) is familiar with angels with wings, faces, hands and feet, wearing robes and holding swords and flowers and playing musical instruments. Similar descriptions of angels can be found in the Bible. Perhaps, of course, these are all anthropomorphic metaphors consistent with the literal immateriality of angels.

Leaving angelology to one side, the important point for present purposes is that if angels have no material bodies then they have no sense organs. Since they have no eyes or ears or noses, it seems that they cannot perceive the world in any way similar to us earthly mortals. For certain followers of Aristotle, such as Aquinas and other medieval scholastics, angels did not even have the power of imagination, for they thought imagination, like sensation, is a bodily process. On this immaterialist interpretation of the angelic mind, angels are pure rational intellects whose minds are devoid of all sensuous experience; or at least they are so until they descend to earth to communicate with humans, at which point perhaps they become able to receive and process streams of sensory information by being temporarily attached or 'housed' in a material body. Indeed, according to scholastic theological tradition, since angels do not have bodies they must borrow unused ones in order to deliver messages to earth. It is important to realize just how puzzling the nature of such a mind would be if there were such a thing. Is an angelic mind like the mind of a creature all of whose sense organs have completely ceased to function, which are 'turned off' either permanently or from time to time, who enters and exits states of total sensory deprivation, like a more extreme version of Helen Keller, who was born deaf, dumb and blind?

It is not clear that this is the right way to think about it. After all, angelic minds, according to the immaterialist interpretation, are not only ones that never or rarely have sensory experiences; they were never supposed to have any sensory experiences in the first place, for it is simply not part of their nature to do so. Add to this Aquinas's view that angels do not even use language, except when communicating with humans and things become even more unfathomable. What would such a pure intelligence be like? Is it a completely different type of mentality, so utterly foreign to us that we cannot even imagine what it would be like? And what is it like when an angel, on an earthly mission, becomes temporarily embodied? Does it experience full-blown sensory awareness or is its experience flattened out and 'flavourless', a deprived form of our own? The latter option is explored in Wim Wenders's film *Wings of Desire*, in which an angel faces the dilemma of having eternal life without sensuous experience or a mortal life overflowing with it. His desire to experience human feelings and sensations is so strong that he chooses to renounce his angelhood and accept the inevitability of death. His first course of action with his new mortal coil is to drink a cup of black coffee, which he thoroughly relishes. In contrast, Descartes appears to have thought, despite the apparent agnosticism of the previous quotation, that the mental life of a temporarily embodied angel would have no sensuous phenomenological dimension at all; it would have no sensory experience but would simply make intellectual judgements about the state of its borrowed body. As he said in one of his letters explaining how mind and body are related in humans: 'if an angel were in a human body, he would not have sensations as we do, but would simply perceive the motions which were caused by external objects, and in this would differ from a real man' (Descartes 1985, vol. III, 206). Interestingly, in his essay 'The Disembodied Woman', the neurologist Oliver Sacks (1986) describes a case of someone approaching this condition. Owing to severe inflammation of her nerves the eponymous patient loses her proprioception, her inner sense of the position of her body and limbs – her 'body image' – and has to rely entirely on her visual perception of them in order to perform even the most daily of tasks, such as sitting, standing, walking and eating, things which most people can do with their eyes closed. There is a bewildering variety of views, in both intellectual history and the popular imagination, about the kinds of minds that exist or that could exist and little agreement about what these minds might be like.

Varieties of mental phenomena

We have been considering, in a very general and highly speculative way, what kinds of creatures have minds and wondering what these minds might be like. In doing so, we have made reference to various features or elements of mentality, such as thought, sensation, perception, imagination and emotion. These things seem to be typical examples of mentality. But what else counts as mental?

ACTIVITY

List as many different kinds of mental phenomena as you can, trying to cover as wide a spectrum of mentality as possible. (The reasons you gave for thinking various things had minds in the previous activity will be of use here.) After you have done this, group the items on your list into larger classes of mental phenomena (for example, anger and joy are both *emotions*, and seeing and hearing are both *perceptions*.)

DISCUSSION

Here are some of the kinds of things that might have appeared on your list, grouped into seven classes:

- **Cognition/intellection**
  belief, knowledge, thought, rationality, judgement, inference, deduction, proof, explanation, recognition, realization, memory.
- **Conation/volition/motivation**
  will, intention, purpose, desire, choice, decision, trying, action (in the sense of doing something, such as walking or waving).
- **Perception**
  seeing, hearing, smelling, touching, tasting, kinaesthesia (the sense of bodily motion, as when we know our legs or fingers or tongue are moving just by feeling them move 'from the inside'), proprioception (the sense of bodily position, as when we know whether we are upright or horizontal).

- **Sensation**
  pain (burns, stings, bites, headaches, cuts, toe stubbings, etc.), nausea, tiredness, orgasm, dizziness, numbness, tickles, itches, hangover.
- **Imagination**
  imaging, day-dreaming, supposing, hallucinating, creating, inventing, pretending, fantasizing, making-believe, seeing-as (e.g., seeing a cloud as a face).
- **Emotion/mood**
  anger, jealousy, fear, love, joy, sorrow, admiration, hate, envy, disgust, panic, happiness, sadness, embarrassment, irritation, amusement, lust.
- **Character/personality**
  arrogance, modesty, pride, vanity, generosity, cleverness, wittiness, shyness.

No doubt alternative categorizations are possible and the categories in which I have placed various putative mental phenomena are somewhat arbitrary. They are one way of initially slicing up the mental pie and this division has been done with an eye on the philosophical issues and problems to be discussed in what follows. There are lots of things that do not fit neatly into any of these categories – hope, expectation, wonder, fascination and dreaming, for example. Some of these may well be in some sense combinations of more primitive and simpler cognitive and conative elements, though we will not pursue such an analysis here. It is tempting to put dreaming under the category of imagination. I have resisted this because the imagination seems largely under our control while dreaming clearly is not. Nor is dreaming a straightforward case of sensation or perception since we do not actually sense or perceive the things we dream of. Perhaps dreaming is an eighth category of mentation unto itself.

It is important to note too that the categories probably overlap to a great extent. Emotions are particularly tricky in this regard: many appear to have cognitive, conative and sensational elements. Fear, for example, is usually accompanied by a distinctive kind of unpleasant feeling; but it also has a cognitive component – a judgement about the dangerousness of something – and a conative component – the desire that the thing in question not happen. But it is doubtful that every emotion is simply a separable combination of judgement, desire and sensation. There seems to be something singular about emotions, which prevents an easy analysis of them in terms of other mentalistic categories, even though they involve features common to mental phenomena of other categories. Some emotions, in fact, such as fear, may be among the most phylogenetically and ontogenetically primitive of mental states. Moreover, the boundary between emotions, moods and sensations is probably not very precise. What kind of mental phenomenon is sympathy, for example, or surprise? I have put both under the heading of 'emotion' but on the face of it they seem to have cognitive, conative and sensational elements.

In short, the categories are intended to be neither exhaustive nor mutually exclusive; they are a way of achieving the generality required in order to pursue a philosophical investigation into the mind. They may need to be revised in the light of further investigation. We may even have to contemplate the possibility that not all of our mental concepts are fully coherent. Moreover, it may well be that not all of them refer to processes or events or states in the same way, or to the same degree or even at all. Dreaming, for example, exhibits a certain peculiarity. On the one hand, we tend to think that people who are asleep are unconscious; when they wake up they come back into consciousness. On the other hand, we also want to say that dreaming is an example of our consciousness in action, since there seems to be some sense in which we are aware of what is going on in us during our dreams.

This brings us to a final point. Neither *consciousness* nor *experience* appears on my list (though they may well have appeared on yours). This may seem odd since they are quintessentially mental phenomena. The reason for their absence is that they are terms even more general than the seven categories above. Indeed, some philosophers think, as Descartes seems to have, that the entire mental realm is itself the realm of consciousness and experience. We need not accept this view, however, to admit that experience is an even more general category than the seven, for it is clear that it encompasses many of the mental phenomena grouped under the various categories. Perceiving, sensing, thinking; having an emotion or being in a certain kind mood – these are all different kinds of experience. An experience is an occurrence that we undergo and for any experience, there is always, in the words of the contemporary American philosopher Thomas Nagel (b.1937), 'something it is like' to have that experience. In other words, experiences have a distinctive kind of *phenomenology*. When I gaze upon a sunset, for example, I have a certain kind of experience, a visual experience. If I close my eyes, or don a pair of sunglasses, my visual experience, what things are like for me visually, changes; when I open my eyes or remove the sunglasses my visual experience is transformed again. It is important, however, not to restrict the notion of phenomenology to the having of *sensory* experience, for there is equally something it is like simply to be thinking about things, as the insomniac knows all too well. It is important too, always to pay close attention to how mental terms are used. Some philosophers use the term 'experience' in a way that does not imply any phenomenology, any 'what-it-is-likeness', and when they want to talk about experiences that do have a phenomenology they say '*conscious* experience'. In this book I shall always use the term 'experience' to imply phenomenology and use the phrase 'conscious experience' as merely an emphatic pleonasm for 'experience'.

What is the connection between consciousness and experience? This is a difficult question, not only because 'consciousness', like 'mental', is an exceedingly slippery term meaning different things to different people, but also because even if we manage to settle on one meaning of the term there are still radically divergent opinions about the nature of consciousness, given the univocal meaning in question. If a being is conscious, in one common sense of the term 'conscious', then it must be having some kind of (sensory or cognitive) experience with a distinctive phenomenology. To be a conscious being is necessarily to be an experiencing being. After all, it does not seem possible for one to be conscious but to be experiencing nothing (O'Shaughessy 2000, 38). The converse may not hold, however: it may be possible to be experiencing something when one is not conscious. Herein may lie the beginnings of an answer to our earlier conundrum about dreaming: perhaps dreams are experiences we have when we are not conscious. Just what we need to add to bare experience to get consciousness is a deep and difficult question that we cannot pursue here. It is important, however, to distinguish consciousness from self-consciousness. As the term suggests, 'self-consciousness' is, roughly speaking, one's consciousness of one's own experience or of one's own self, or the ability to become so conscious. Thus, when I am self-conscious, I attend to my own experiences and think about myself. I may notice that my eyesight is getting worse or I may wonder whether I am really any good at philosophy. The distinction between consciousness and self-consciousness allows us to say, plausibly, that some animals are conscious but not self-conscious; that is, they have experiences, whether of their own bodily states or external goings-on, but cannot *reflect* upon their own experiences.

The attitudinal and the experiential

ACTIVITY

Are there any mental phenomena that do not involve having an experience?

DISCUSSION

Though the term 'experience' covers a lot of the mental territory, it does not seem to cover it all. Having a belief, for example, does not seem to be any kind of experience, nor does having an intention or a memory. There does not seem to be anything it is like to believe that Descartes was a Christian or to remember that he was; such a thing does not have much 'feel' to it or any kind of distinctive phenomenology. Similarly, wanting something and intending to do something do not seem to be different kinds of experiences that we undergo. After all, you can want something, intend to do something and believe something all while you are in a dreamless sleep.

Philosophers call beliefs, wants, and intentions *attitudes* because they all involve having a certain kind of attitude toward something; they all involve what is sometimes called 'direction upon something'. One can have various different attitudes toward, for example, the state of affairs in which Descartes is a Christian: one can believe it, desire it, fear it, lament it and so on. When one does so, one's attitude is directed at or focused upon something, in this case, upon the state of affairs in which Descartes is a Christian. This *attitudinal direction upon an object* is called 'intentionality' and attitudes are often called 'intentional states' and are said to possess 'intentionality'. The term 'intentionality' has a long and complex history stretching back through the medieval scholastics and ultimately to Aristotle. It derives from the medieval Latin word '*intention*', which literally means a tension or stretching towards, and is used by the scholastics as a term for the mind's direction upon the objects of thought. The British philosopher Elizabeth Anscombe (b.1919) has speculated that it was chosen because of an analogy between stretching towards and aiming one's bow at something and aiming one's thought at something. Attitudes such as belief and desire have intentionality because they point beyond themselves to something else, and this something else is sometimes called the 'intentional object' of the attitude. Sometimes the thing towards which an attitude is directed is called the 'content' of the attitude. So philosophers sometimes say that the content of my belief or desire or fear that Descartes was a Christian is that *Descartes was a Christian.* Employing this term, we can say that one can have different attitudes to the same content: one can believe the content, dispute the content, fear the content, and so on. (One should always be aware of subtly different ways of using this terminology. Some philosophers distinguish between the content of an attitude and the intentional object of the attitude. In the case of belief, the intentional object is whatever thing the belief is about and the content is what it is that is believed about the object. For example, using this terminology, the intentional object of my belief that Descartes was a Christian is *Descartes himself* – for it is Descartes I am thinking of – and the content of my belief – i.e. *what it is* that I believe about him – is *that he is a Christian.*)

One of the most interesting and perplexing things about attitudes is that they appear to be capable of being directed at things that do not exist. Thus in the late nineteenth century many anthropologists had beliefs about the so-called 'Piltdown Man', even though the eponymous fossils turned out to be an elaborate hoax, cobbled together out of bits of human and orang-utan skulls. Small children have beliefs about Santa Claus and physicists about 'phlogiston' (a substance once falsely believed to be released into the air during combustion). But if none of these things exists, if there is no Piltdown Man, no Santa Claus or phlogiston, then how can we have thoughts about them? What is it that our thoughts are about in such cases, since we appear to be thinking about, directing our thoughts upon, things that do not exist?

As we noted earlier, some attitudes, such as belief, do not seem to have an experiential component. Some, of course, do: very strong desires, such as sexual lust, for example, and expectation and being startled. Conversely, many experiential mental phenomena have an attitudinal element, in the sense that, like belief, they are directed at things. Fear and disgust are obviously directed upon certain things and states of affairs – we are typically afraid *of* something and disgusted *at* something – as well as having an essential visceral element to them. Perception, too, is directed: we always see something or hear something. Whether sensations such as pain, nausea and orgasm have an attitudinal or 'intentional' component is, however, controversial.

ACTIVITY

Intentionality is a complex and controversial topic and we shall return to it in more detail later. Before leaving the notion, however, consider the following question.

Does pain have an attitudinal component, that is, does it point to something beyond itself in the way that beliefs do? In other words, are pains *about anything* in the way that beliefs are about things?

DISCUSSION

There is a tendency to think of pain as entirely a pure 'raw feel', a distinctively unpleasant feeling, *painfulness*. But it is also very plausible to think of pain as an indication of bodily damage, as pointing to a distressed area of the body, especially when evolutionary considerations are in the forefront. Pain, then, seems to have both experiential and attitudinal sides to it. Some philosophers would argue, however, that this indicator feature of pain, while extremely important to an animal's survival, is not an essential feature of pain and that the real essence of pain, what makes pain pain, is its experiential character, its painfulness. After all, if evolution had instead unfolded so that a tickling sensation was the indicator of bodily damage, then this ticklish sensation would not be pain. Conversely, if for some reason, sensations of pain were not in any way indicators of bodily damage they would nevertheless still be pain.

Wherever the truth of the matter lies with respect to pain, the distinction between the attitudinal and the experiential side of the mental is a very useful one and we shall have recourse to it in much of what follows. The attitudinal and experiential seem to be two poles of a spectrum on which one can situate mental phenomena (cf. Guttenplan 2000). Some mental phenomena seem to lie close to one end because they are virtually all attitude, as it were, such as belief; some lie near the other extreme, being all but experience, such as pain, while others lie somewhere nearer the middle, possessing both attitudinal and experiential features, such as fear and disgust (with their intentional and visceral sides).

Dispositions versus occurrences

Another important distinction to keep in mind is that between what philosophers call *dispositions* and what they call *occurrences*. A disposition is a tendency or propensity to manifest or exhibit something in certain circumstances. A wine glass, for example, has the dispositional property of brittleness: it will shatter into pieces when struck with enough force. But it need not ever actually shatter for it to possess the disposition of brittleness (it may be melted down into something else before it has a chance to shatter). Solubility and conductivity are other examples. Aspirins are soluble and copper wires conduct electricity – even though some aspirins will never make contact with water and even though not every copper wire will encounter an electric charge. The actual shattering of the wine glass, the dissolving of the aspirin, and the conducting of the copper wire, if such things end up happening, are all occurrences: they are events or processes that happen at certain times and have a certain continuous duration. The distinction between dispositions and occurrences applies also to mental phenomena, though not quite as straightforwardly as it does to glass, aspirin and copper. Many beliefs, for example, appear to be dispositional in nature, such as the belief that dogs are not explosive. Anyone who knows anything about dogs knows they are not explosive but the thought has probably never occurred to you before now. Nevertheless, that you did believe this before it occurred to you is clear from the fact that you have petted dogs without a second thought and this behaviour of yours was not considered reckless abandon. Many beliefs are like this: the belief that the chair you are sitting on will support your weight, or that the floor of your house will not cave in, that your car is not made of mud, that Descartes never met Darwin and so on. These beliefs are dispositional in the sense that they are not events or processes that we undergo; rather, they lead to or manifest themselves in the production of certain kinds of occurrences, such as the petting of dogs, the sitting on of chairs and the acknowledging of the fact that Descartes never met Darwin when confronted with it. Pain, nausea, being startled, perceiving and thinking are events or processes – occurrences – that we undergo.

The relations among mental phenomena

> There is no escaping the fact that want of sympathy condemns us to a corresponding stupidity. Mephistopheles thrown upon real life, and obliged to manage his own plots, would inevitably make blunders.
>
> (George Eliot, *Adam Bede*)

We have seen that it seems natural to say that while it is possible for machines and angels to have intellects superior to ours, it is also natural to say that they will be subject, to far less extent, to that range of sensuous, perceptual and emotional experiences that infuses human mental life – and even perhaps to no extent at all. This raises the question of what the relation is among the various mental phenomena. Consider reason and emotion, for example. It is common to think that thought or reason is a relatively autonomous feature of the mental, in the sense that it can operate successfully in a creature without emotion. Indeed, the idea of a purely rational creature unadulterated by any emotion is one often contemplated by philosophers and lay people alike as not only a possibility but the kind of creature we should positively strive to become. But just how independent of emotion is rationality really? Recent research in neuroscience has begun to cast some doubt on the idea that rationality, at least our rationality, is an autonomous domain that can function independently of emotion. It seems that an absence or distortion of normal emotional functioning can lead to breakdowns in rationality. People who suffer certain kinds of damage to those parts of the brain thought to control and regulate emotional responses often have serious problems making decisions, forming plans and generally organizing their life in a safe and successful way. Some neuroscientists think that emotional states, which appear to be subserved by neural mechanisms in certain areas of the brain, bias or 'colour' certain of our memories, experiences and thoughts by 'marking' them with degrees of urgency and calm, which have the effect of driving certain thoughts into our attention and pushing others away. Emotions may be the wheels of thought, allowing us to concentrate on important things without being swamped with too much ultimately irrelevant information.

Much of the evidence for the interconnection between the various aspects of our mental life comes from the investigation of people with brain damage and mental illnesses. Among the more extreme types of mental illness is the Capgras delusion, and reflection upon it suggests another possible link between different types of mental phenomena, this time between emotion and perception. Capgras patients believe that a close relative – usually a spouse or parent – has been replaced by an impostor who looks exactly like the replaced person. Depending on the background knowledge of the patients, the impostor may be thought by them to be a robot or a clone. The delusion is relatively circumscribed in the sense that the subjects do not integrate the delusional belief with the rest of their knowledge about how the world works. For example, they do not initiate searches for the people who they think have been replaced and do not contact the police; indeed, they seem relatively uninterested in the location or fate of their spouses or parents. The patients' reaction to the 'impostor' can be friendly but is often antagonistic. That the delusional belief is sincerely held, and that the subjects are not 'faking it', is borne out by the fact that the delusion is sometimes accompanied by violent behaviour against the 'impostor' who can appear malevolent or evil to the patient. One man with the Capgras delusion decapitated his stepfather, whom he believed to be a robot, in order to find the batteries and microchips he thought would be in his head. Another Capgras patient stabbed and shot both her parents.

One of the most promising lines of explanation for this sad and disturbing delusion is that the patients in question form the delusional belief in order to explain a very strange and anomalous perceptual experience they undergo when they see the relatives in question. The idea is that Capgras patients have lost the increased emotional or affective responses that normally accompany the perception of familiar faces but have retained the separate capacity to recognize them. The 'impostor hypothesis' is an attempt to explain this very peculiar perceptual experience of seeing a person exactly like your spouse, say, but oddly feeling no affection or emotional attachment towards him or her. (This is similar to what seems to be happening to people in the early eerie part of the '50s science-fiction thriller *Invasion of the Body Snatchers*, in which townspeople begin to think that some of their closest relations have been replaced by duplicates or clones.) This is supported to a certain extent by the fact that when some Capgras patients speak to the person in question on the phone they do not think that they are speaking to an impostor but to the real person, the very person who, when seen by them, they think is an impostor. In these cases, it is only their visual experience that is drained of emotional significance; their auditory experience remains suffused with emotional import.

In another type of bizarre case, the Cotard delusion, patients sometimes think that they are dead. This seems to be another type of reaction to undergoing strange perceptual experiences that are drained of emotional significance owing to an even more pervasive flattening of affective response to perceptual stimuli. These absent or reduced affective or emotional responses have a significant impact on perceptual experiences themselves and, ultimately, on thoughts and judgements. The upshot is that the emotions may be intimately involved in the proper functioning of perception.

Yet another baffling type of psychopathology is described by Sacks (1986) in his book *The Man Who Mistook His Wife for a Hat* and suggests a possible link between imagination and perception. The eponymous patient, known to us as 'Dr P', has severely, but very oddly, impaired perceptual abilities. Though he has no deterioration in any of his other mental abilities (he is a very talented musician), he can no longer recognize his students or identify members of his family from photographs. He cannot recognize the sexes of people on the television or their emotional expressions. He regularly confuses animate objects, such as his wife's head, with inanimate ones, such as his hat (he tries to 'put on' his wife's head thinking it is his hat). He can no longer recognize everyday objects, such as flowers, shoes and gloves. When asked by Sacks to identify a glove Dr P responds with: 'a continuous surface infolded on itself [which] appears to have five outpouchings'. It seems as if Sacks's musician has lost the capacity to understand or interpret or categorize his own visual experiences even though he can describe in strikingly intelligent detail, using sophisticated geometrical concepts, what they are like. But exactly which aspect of his mentality has become impaired or is 'missing'? It appears to be neither his rationality nor his visual perception. Could some of his imaginative abilities have somehow become debilitated? Although he can see a pair of gloves in all its geometrical detail he can no longer see them *as gloves*, the way we can see them as gloves or the way that, as Shakespeare's Antony puts it,

Sometime we see a cloud that's dragonish;
A vapour sometime like a bear or lion,
A towered citadel, a pendent rock,
A forked mountain or blue promontory
With trees upon't that nod unto the world
And mock our eyes with air.

For Sacks's poor Dr P, however, the situation is lamentably like that in which Antony thinks he finds himself:

That which is now a horse, even with a thought
The rack dislimns, and makes it indistinct,
As water is in water.

(*Antony and Cleopatra*, Act 4, Scene 14)

It is even worse than this, of course, for Dr P; for him the identities of even ordinary objects have become 'dislimned'. Ludwig Wittgenstein (1889–1951) notes that

> We do not see facial contortions and make inferences from them (like a doctor framing a diagnosis) to joy, grief, boredom. We describe a face immediately as sad, radiant, bored, even when we are unable to give any other description of the features. – Grief, one would like to say, is personified in the face.
>
> (Wittgenstein 1967, §225, 41)

It appears that Dr P has lost the capacity for instant recognition and is confined to making inferences from facial contortions to emotions and from the shapes of objects to what kind of objects they are. If certain imaginative abilities are required for seeing-as, and seeing-as required for certain kinds of perceptual experiences – such as visually experiencing emotion personified in a face – then the prospects for building a mechanical device, such as a robot, with perceptual abilities approaching our own may depend on the device in question possessing some kind of imaginative capacity. Again, we are confronted with the possibility of a strong link between what may appear to be autonomous mental phenomena: imagination and perception.

The link between visual experience and perception is no more straightforward, however, than that between imagination and perception. While Dr P may not be able to see certain shapes as kinds of things (as gloves, say) he does at least have visual experiences of shapes and objects; that is, he is aware or conscious of shapes and colours. But there are well-documented cases of people who are, in some sense, able to perceive things that they claim to have utterly no awareness of. This phenomenon, called 'blind sight', occurs in people who have suffered damage to the visual cortex in their brain. They have a blind spot or scotoma, an area of the visual field that is a phenomenological blank. But interestingly, although these people deny they are conscious or aware of anything at all within the region of their scotoma, they can guess what kinds of simply shaped objects or patterns are held before them in the blind spot region when urged to do so and they can do this with an accuracy better than chance. They seem still to be receiving some kind of 'information' or stimulation through their eyes from the objects but are not conscious of it. It seems in these cases that there is still some unconscious processing going on which is divorced from the usually accompanying visual experience.

Summary

We have been primarily concerned to explore in a preliminary fashion the domain of the mental. We have looked briefly at various different kinds of actual and possible minds – normal and abnormal human minds, animal minds, angelic minds, and so on – and at the variety of mental phenomena – thought, perception, sensation, emotion, etc. Describing what a mind might be like is partly a matter of describing the kinds of mental phenomena that the mind in question exhibits. Conceiving of what a possible mind very different from our own might be like, however – the mind of an angel or animal, for example – is very difficult. In fact, it may be more difficult than we think, for as we saw, there may be surprising connections between what might at first sight seem to be relatively autonomous mental phenomena: between emotion and reason, emotion and perception, imagination and perception; as well as very surprising disconnections, for example, in the case of blindsight, between conscious visual experience and unconscious perception. Mind and mental phenomena are obviously very complex indeed and nothing very conclusive can be drawn from our preliminary and pre-theoretical reflections. They are intended as initial forays into the mental territory that we shall be exploring more systematically in the chapters that follow. We noted two important distinctions, however, that can be very helpful when thinking about the complex nature of minds: that between attitudes and experiences and that between dispositions and occurrences. As we shall see, these two distinctions can help us think about the nature of the mental.

We began this chapter by noting the distinction between the living and the non-living, and between the minded and the non-minded. It is a matter of controversy which living creatures in the world fall into the category of the minded. It is also a matter of controversy whether only living things fall into this category. Can machines such as computers and robots have minds? Can purely spiritual beings with no bodies have minds? If so, what could their minds be like? In the next chapter we shall look in more detail at the relation between life and mentality by examining the profound shift in thinking about these matters that occurred during the rise of modern science in the seventeenth century.

Further reading

General introductions to the philosophy of mind tend to be ahistorical and vary greatly in accessibility and coverage. E.J. Lowe covers virtually the whole range of topics in his *An Introduction to the Philosophy of Mind* (2000). For less coverage but more detail see Jaegwon Kim's slightly more advanced but excellent *Philosophy of Mind* (1996). Tim Crane's *The Elements of Mind* (2001) is another very good but more advanced introduction to current issues and contains one of the best recent introductions to the idea of intentionality. Samuel Guttenplan's *Mind's Landscape* (2000) offers a more accessible introduction to intentionality and other aspects of mind and has influenced my own presentation of some of the issues, as has William Lyon's *Matters of Mind* (2001), which is a very readable history of twentieth-century philosophy of mind. Daniel Dennett's *Kinds of Minds* (1996) is a popular introduction to an evolutionary perspective on mind with reflections on animal and robot minds. Two of the best collections of classic and recent essays in the philosophy of mind are *The Nature of Mind*, edited by David Rosenthal (1991) and *Mind and Cognition* (1st and 2nd editions), edited by William Lycan (1990 and 1999). Those interested in the history of the concept of mind and the etymology of 'mind' and related words in various ancient and modern languages should consult Paul MacDonald's *History of the Concept of Mind. Speculations about Soul, Mind and Spirit from Homer to Hume* (2003). Fascinating discussions of disorders of mind can be found in the works of several neurologists and neuroscientists, such as V.S. Ramachandran's Reith Lectures *The Emerging Mind* (2003) and Ramachandran and Sandra Blakeslee's, *Phantoms in the Brain* (1998). See also Antonio Damasio's *Descartes's Error* (1994), which investigates the link between emotion and rationality, and Oliver Sacks's *The Man Who Mistook His Wife for a Hat* (1986), a collection of short literary essays on case histories.

CHAPTER 2

From Rationality to Consciousness: Descartes's Concept of Mind

And new philosophy calls all in doubt,
The element of fire is quite put out;
The sun is lost and th'earth, and no man's wit
Can well direct him where to look for it.

(John Donne, 'Anatomy of the World', 1611)

The focus of this chapter is the radical change in thinking about the nature of the human mind and the human body epitomized by Descartes and the general Cartesianism that swept through Christian Europe during the Enlightenment, in particular in the early seventeenth century. This period of history is characterized by the rise of a 'new philosophy', namely, the beginnings of modern astronomy and the mathematical-cum-mechanical view of the workings of nature, pioneered by Copernicus, Galileo, Descartes and others, which gradually replaced the older Aristotelian tradition. As we shall see, the new mechanism had profound effects on how the minds and bodies of human and other animals were understood.

Aristotelianism

ACTIVITY

Read the first half of G.B. Matthews' article 'Consciousness and life', Reading 1, Part I, pages 122–30.

1 What line of reasoning does Matthews describe as 'Aristotelian'?

2 In what way does Descartes break with Aristotelianism, according to Matthews?

DISCUSSION

1. The Aristotelian reasoning Matthews refers to is this: inferring that Tik-Tok is not conscious, or does not think, that is, has no mentality, from the premise that Tik-Tok is not alive. We have distinguished between the attitudinal and experiential sides of mentality. Let us follow Matthews, however, and set aside the issue of the connection between thought (attitude) and consciousness (experience), for the moment. The question Matthews is interested in is the connection between *mentality* and life, though he uses the terms 'thought' and 'consciousness'. Given that he is not interested in distinguishing between thought and consciousness (attitude and experience) we can take him to be talking about the broad category of the mental and comparing the Aristotelian account of the relation between mentality and life and the Cartesian conception of the relation between them.
2. According to Matthews, Descartes breaks with traditional Aristotelianism by rejecting both the connection between life and consciousness and the separation of life and mechanism.

Let us look in more detail at the nature of Aristotelianism or the 'Peripatetic' philosophy, as it is sometimes called, supposedly after the *peripatos* or covered walk in the Lyceum around which Aristotle and his students strolled as he taught. In Aristotle's metaphysics, all individual things have both *form* and *matter*. Roughly speaking, the matter is the stuff out of which something is composed and the form is the way the matter is structured and organized or, in some cases, the form is the kind of activity distinctive of the thing in question or the function of the thing in question. The basic idea is that it is in virtue of a thing's form that is has the properties and dispositions it has, that it exhibits the characteristic behaviour it does. The characteristic type of behaviour may be relatively static or a dynamic feature responsible for change. In some cases, the form of something is connected to its function, that is, its end or purpose. A statue, for example, consists of some material, such as bronze or marble, and this is cast or carved into a certain shape, such as a bust of Aristotle perhaps. The bronze is the matter and the shape is the form. The form of a seed, however, is its power or capacity to grow into a particular kind of tree. A house is a load of timber and bricks arranged in a certain way that provides shelter; the timber and bricks are the matter and its function as a shelter is its form. The form of something determines what *kind* of thing it is. The form of a statue is its shape, that of a seed its capacity to grow into a tree and that of a house its function as a shelter. This is the doctrine of *hylomorphism* (from the Greek *hyle* for matter and *morphe* for shape or form).

For Aristotle and his later followers, such St Thomas Aquinas and other medieval scholastics, although all individual things have forms, there is a sharp distinction between the form of living (animate) things and the form of non-living (inanimate) things, in that the form of a living thing – that which makes it into a living thing – is the *soul*. As Matthews notes, there is no term in ancient Greek equivalent to 'conscious'; in fact, there is no obvious equivalent of 'mind' or 'mental' either. The central concept in Aristotle's discussion of living creatures is *psyché* (Latin: *anima*), which is standardly translated as 'soul'. From *psyché* we have derived 'psychology', 'psychological' and their cognates. For Aristotle the *psyché* or the soul is the form of a living organism. The soul is essentially that in virtue of which an organism is alive. On this biological conception of the soul, plants and spiders have souls. The soul is simply the animating 'principle of life' associated with the characteristic activities of living things. This is very different from the theological view of the soul with which we are more familiar. According to Aristotelians, there is an ordered hierarchy of souls. At the lowest level is the nutritive or *vegetative soul*, associated with the activities of nutrition, reproduction and growth. Thus plants have vegetative souls. Animals, however, are differentiated from plants by their capacities for sense perception, appetite, emotion and locomotion, which are owed to their possession of *sensitive souls*. Birds and cats, for example, cannot only take nourishment and reproduce, but can move and see and feel and remember. At the top level of the hierarchy we find human beings who have the additional capacity for intellection or rational thought (in ancient Greek, *noûs*, which is also often confusingly translated as 'mind'). Humans thus have intelligent or *rational souls*, since they engage in the activities of judging and reasoning.

Form cannot exist without matter. Without some bronze or marble or other material, there can be no statue; without timber and bricks or other materials, there can be no shelter. Similarly, a soul, which is the form of a living organism, cannot exist without a body; indeed, a soul is simply the characteristic activities or functions of living bodies, just as a shelter is the function provided by a particular arrangement of timber and bricks. A dead body has no soul because it has ceased to function in the manner constitutive of living things; it no longer moves of its own accord, metabolizes, senses or thinks. A body that is a corpse has a different form from that same body when it is alive. Importantly, there is no sensation, perception, imagination and emotion without a body. Whether, for Aristotle, there can be thought (in our sense of attitude) without body is a controversial exegetical question, as Matthews indicates. Although Aristotle is notoriously unclear about this, Matthews takes his official line to be that no psychological or mental powers can exist apart from a body, including thinking. (We will return to the all-important question of the relation between thinking and matter in detail in the final chapter.)

So, in denying that a machine, such as the mechanical man Tik-Tok, can think (or be conscious – remember that at this point we are interested in mentality broadly conceived) on the basis of the claim that a machine is not alive, the philosopher Ziff is relying on an Aristotelian connection between psychological capacities and activities on the one hand and life on the other. Just as Aristotle thought only living things had souls, so Ziff thinks that only living things can have mentality (can think or be conscious). Moreover, Ziff is relying on an Aristotelian separation between life and mechanism: artefacts and machines are not alive.

The claims:

1 If Tik-Tok is not alive then he cannot be conscious

2 If Tik-Tok is a mechanism then he cannot be alive

are said by Ziff to be a part of the 'semantical rules' of English, that is, the rules governing the meanings of words or sentences in English. Just as it is part of the semantical rules of English that 'sister' means 'female sibling', so too, Ziff is claiming, it is part of semantical rules of English that the word 'conscious' includes 'is alive' as part of its meaning.

Matthews says that talk about semantical rules can be expressed in terms of *entailment*. Entailment is a transitive relation, which means that if one thing entails another, and that second thing entails a third thing, then the first thing entails the third. So if Ziff claims that '*x* is a mechanism' entails '*x* is not alive' and '*x* is not alive' entails '*x* is not conscious', he is committed to the claim that '*x* is a mechanism' entails '*x* is not conscious'. So it follows that 'Tik-Tok is a mechanism' entails 'Tik-Tok is not conscious'. This means that it is impossible for Tik-Tok to be conscious because it is impossible that machines be conscious (and Tik-Tok is a machine). Ziff's idea is that a machine can no more be conscious than a sister can be a male sibling. It is part of the very meaning or definition of the word 'sister' that sisters are female siblings. Another way of putting this is to say that it is necessarily true that sisters are female siblings. A *necessary truth* is one that cannot possibly be false. That 9+1=10, that squares have four sides and that sisters are female siblings are all necessary truths because they cannot possibly be false. So, what Ziff is saying is that it is a necessary truth that Tik-Tok is not conscious; because Tik-Tok is a mechanism, it follows from the meaning of 'mechanism' that he is not conscious. Once we have established that Tik-Tok is indeed a mechanism we do not need to carry out any further empirical investigation of him to conclude that he cannot be conscious. To say that Tik-Tok is a conscious machine would be self-contradictory in the same way that saying Tik-Tok is a male sister is self-contradictory. Some truths about Tik-Tok are not necessary; for example, his being fitted with a 'special clockwork attachment'. That is a *contingent truth* because it can possibly be false. Tik-Tok could have been fitted with some other attachment or no attachment at all. Similarly, that the Earth has one moon and that Descartes died in Sweden are contingent truths because they might have been false; the Earth could have had more than one moon and Descartes might have died in the Netherlands

If it is true that thinking machines are impossible then many science-fiction stories are contradictory. You may think this is a harsh verdict to pronounce on such science-fiction writers as Isaac Asimov and Robert Heinlein, for while their robots are fictional, they do not seem to be *impossible*; it is not as if they are writing about characters who are male sisters. If you agree that Tik-Tok is not alive or conscious but that it is possible he could be, then you must reject Ziff's claim that the connection between 'conscious' and 'living' is a necessary one. On this view, the connection between life and conscious is contingent. Similarly, you might have thought that the reason why Tik-Tok cannot think or be alive, if indeed he cannot, is that, as a matter of contingent fact about the nature of the world, silicon-based artefacts cannot support life or consciousness and that only organic processes can. It may well be, then, that the reason why Tik-Tok cannot think is that it is a contingent truth that no machine can think in the same way that it is a contingent truth that Tik-Tok has a 'special clockwork attachment'. In short, then, both Ziff and Aristotle agree on the connection between life and mentality, and on the separation of life and mechanism. It is possible, however, to view the status of the connection and separation differently. While for Ziff and Aristotle it is necessary, others might think it is merely contingent. We should note finally that one could hold that whether a machine could have mentality is contingent alright and, moreover, it is true! Tik-Tok does in fact have a mind. Though we do not now have thinking machines like Tik-Tok we might well have sometime in the future.

Life, mind and mechanism: the Cartesian view

> As regards the animals, Descartes was the first who, with a boldness worthy of reverence, ventured to think of the animal as a *machine*.
>
> (Nietzsche, *The Anti-Christ*, §14)

Descartes breaks with traditional Aristotelianism by rejecting both the connection between life and consciousness and the separation of life and mechanism. Where the Aristotelians placed a divide between living and non-living bodies, Descartes postulates a continuum. The way in which living organisms operate is no different from how non-living things operate, whether they are natural objects like rocks and waterfalls or artificial ones like clocks and mills. Indeed, for Descartes, living animal bodies, including the human body, are machines all of whose powers and functions can be explained on the basis of mechanical principles. As he says, there is no reason to postulate any vegetative, sensitive or locomotive soul, or any other 'principle of life', to explain the functioning of the human or any other animal body. All of physical nature is one big mechanism operating according to mathematically expressible laws. As many commentators have pointed out, Descartes took inspiration from the mechanical statues in the royal gardens of his day. As he says in to his readers in the *Treatise on Man*:

> you may have observed in the grottos and fountains in the royal gardens that the mere force with which the water is driven as it emerges is sufficient to move various machines, and even to make them play certain instruments or utter certain words depending on the various arrangements of the pipes through which the water is conducted... visitors who enter the grottos of these fountains... unwittingly cause the movements which take place before their eyes. For they cannot enter without stepping on certain tiles which are so arranged that if, for example, they approach Diana who is bathing they will cause her to hide in the reeds, and if they move forward to pursue her they will cause Neptune to advance and threaten them with his trident; or if they go in another direction they will cause a sea-monster to emerge and spew water onto their faces; or other such things according to the whim of the engineers who made the fountain.
>
> (Descartes 1985, vol. I, 101)

Animal bodies, of course, are far, far more complex mechanisms, being the work of the greatest engineer of all, God.

Importantly for Descartes, however, there is one power or capacity that cannot be explained by mechanical principles and cannot therefore be a property of any kind of body whether natural or artificial: thought (in the broad sense of mentality). Thought is the activity of an immaterial substance that is joined or united with a material body for a certain period of time. On Descartes's view there is no reason why an immaterial soul or mind could not be united with a machine, such as Tik-Tok the Mechanical Man; in fact, our minds are united to a kind of machine, for that is what our bodies are, although they are natural rather than artificial machines. Thus Descartes severs the connection between thought or consciousness – mentality in general – and life precisely because he severs the connection between thought and body. Since it is not bodies that think in the first place, yet only bodies can be alive, there is no essential connection between thought and life.

Descartes's metaphysical framework is thus very different from the preceding Aristotelian one. Since the medieval scholastic philosophers generally adopted the Aristotelian framework, according to which there is a necessary connection between mentality and life and a separation of life and mechanism, the term 'soul' came to be used in a way that embodied this framework. Since the soul is the seat of thought and mentality, and the soul is the form of a living body, thought or mentality is essentially tied to a living body. Thus, the meaning of the term 'soul', and with it various other mentalistic terms, became locked together in meaning with 'life'. So Matthews speaks of Ziff's Aristotelian claim that there is a 'conceptual connection' between consciousness and life (and a conceptual incompatibility between life and mechanism). In order for Descartes to express his radically different metaphysical view he must use mentalistic terms in a different way; he must give a new meaning to them, namely, one according to which there is no 'semantical' or necessary connection with life and living bodies.

Christian Aristotelianism and thinking as an immaterial process

Before we turn to Descartes's reasons for wanting to adopt his new view we must pause to consider an important development in the metaphysics of mind that took place between Aristotle and Descartes, during the medieval period in which Christian thought dominated philosophy in western Europe.

The Aristotelian doctrine of hylomorphism formed the metaphysical basis of philosophical thought in the Christian Middle Ages. But Christian philosophers and theologians faced a central problem of reconciling Aristotelian hylomorphism with the Christian doctrine of the immortality of the soul. It is obvious what the problem is: if the soul is the form of the living body then when the body dies the soul can no longer exist, just as the form of a house – namely, shelter – cannot exist once the timber and bricks have crumbled away. So, if the soul is the form of a living human body, then how can the soul be immortal, how can it survive the death of the body?

Aquinas's way out of this problem is to claim that while the nutritive and sensitive powers of living things depend on the body, the rational or intellectual powers do not. While sight and hearing are dependent on bodily organs, the eyes and ears, the rational capacities can operate independently of any body. The rational soul's independence of body is unique and is called 'subsistence' by Aquinas; the rational soul or rational part of the soul 'subsists' when the body is dead and decayed. (As we have already seen, this separation of thought and intellection from sensation and perception is not unprecedented. Even Aristotle seems to wonder, somewhat inconclusively, whether the power of thought (*noûs*) might exist apart from body.) Indeed, Aristotle's teacher Plato had already taught that the rational part of the soul is immortal and in fact eternal. Aquinas differed from Plato in holding that while the rational soul (or rational part of the soul) was immortal it was not eternal: God creates the rational soul of each individual and implants it in his or her body when he or she first appears on earth. When the body of an individual dies, its rational soul – which consists of the intellect and the will – subsists for a time independently of any body and is eventually reunited with it when the body is resurrected. What survives the death of the body is something much less than the full mental life of a normal embodied human being. For in their subsistent states immortal souls cannot sense or imagine since these require bodily organs. Interestingly, in light of this, Aquinas held that the immortal soul is less than a full person and that therefore in order for there to be personal immortality, that is, in order for *you* to be immortal, the rational soul had to be joined again with the body after the resurrection. Thus the personal immortality of each individual human being depends essentially on bodily resurrection, though part of us – our rational souls, that is, our intellects and wills – survive for a time without our bodies, awaiting resurrection. In fact, for Aquinas, the intellectual soul must be attached to a body in order to acquire knowledge because, unlike the higher intellectual substances, such as angels, the human intellectual soul has no innate knowledge built into it from the beginning of its creation. The only way it can acquire knowledge is by being fed sensory data through the sense organs of a corporeal substance upon which the intellect acts to form judgements. Thus the very character of the intellectual soul is formed by its union with the body. What appears to happen in the development of thought about the soul after Aristotle is that there is a gradual shift away from the Aristotelian notion of the soul as a set of capacities and activities and a shift back to a more Platonic view of the soul as literally an entity. This, of course, accords well with the Christian belief that the soul survives the death of the body and is certainly more in tune with how we now think of the soul.

Accounting for the immortality of the soul, however, is not the only reason for thinking that the power of thought is not a bodily process. The very nature of thought itself, that is, of intellectual activities like judging, seemed to many ancient philosophers and to the medieval scholastics, to demand that it be immaterial. This is because thought involves the capacity for grasping 'universals', such as *humanity, doghood, rabbithood, causality* and *justice* and any number of other properties that many things can share. Since these shared qualities of things are not material, and since the intellect can think about other things that are not material, such as the abstract objects of logic and mathematics – numbers, for example – it must itself be immaterial. This argument relies on what we would consider an obscure principle accepted by the ancients and scholastics: namely, that the knower must be the same kind of thing as, or homogeneous with, the known, or else never the twain shall meet. Non-human animals, with their purely corporeal sensitive souls, can perceive individual corporeal things: a dog can see and smell rabbits and other dogs. But a dog cannot have knowledge of higher mathematics or universal concepts such as *rabbit*, because these things are abstract and immaterial and there is nothing in the dog – or in any merely animal soul – that is immaterial. This view was buttressed for these philosophers by there seeming to be no clear *organ* of thought in the way in which there clearly are organs of sense. So the idea that thinking itself must be an immaterial process was considered by many to be entirely plausible.

Two points of note emerge from this discussion. First, though the Aristotelians and Thomists placed humans in a continuum with animals and plants, in virtue of all of them possessing a soul, they distinguished humankind from the animals by the former's possession of a rational soul. In other words, what distinguishes us from the animals is our capacity for intellection, volition and rationality. When it comes to sensory experience – to sensing, perceiving, imagining and having emotions – we are, so to speak, on all fours with the beasts. The defining feature of the human mind is, then, intellect and will, the abilities to judge and take decisions – in short, rationality. One way of expressing this would be to say that what marks us off from the animals is our possession of a mind. In saying this one would be drawing the boundaries of the mind around the rational faculties of thought and decision. The idea is that if mind is rationality, then, so far as we know, at the present, only human beings have minds, properly speaking. Animals have no minds; their capacities for sense perception bestow upon them only a 'vegetative soul'. In order to have a mind, a creature needs a rational soul, a capacity for conceptual thought, an ability to grasp universals. One reaction to this is to say that it amounts to a mere stipulation about how to use the term 'mind'. The response to this reaction is that it misses an important point: namely, that according to a long standing philosophical tradition, what is special about human mentality is its essential capacity for rationality – and that is something, whatever you want to call it, which we do not share with the beasts (though Hume, of course, disagrees). In addition, this power of thought, which distinguishes us from mere animals, is immaterial and immortal. With this background in mind, let us turn back to Descartes's radical break with his Aristotelian and Thomist predecessors.

Descartes's concept of mind

ACTIVITY

Read the second half of the Matthews article, Reading 1, Part II, pp.130–5.

Why, according to Matthews, does Descartes think that there is no entailment from '*x* is conscious' to '*x* is alive'?

DISCUSSION

Descartes thinks that one cannot infer '*x* is alive' from '*x* is conscious' (or from '*x* has a mind') because he thinks it is possible to be conscious or have a mind without having a body. Since a body is required for something to be alive, it follows that it must be possible for mentality to exist without being alive. This immediately raises the question of why Descartes thinks it is possible for the mind to exist without the body. He offers a number of famous and fascinating arguments for what he calls 'the Real Distinction between mind and body'. Matthews emphasizes one such argument, which is sometimes called the argument from doubt. Crudely put, the argument begins with the premise that, as Matthews puts it, 'what he is, what really and truly belongs to him, is something that he cannot doubt belongs to him' (p.130); since he can doubt whether he has a body, his body does not really and truly belong to him, it is not part of his essential nature. It must rather be something in which he is temporarily housed – if it even exists at all, for Descartes famously thinks that it is possible for a powerful evil demon to trick him into thinking he has a body when in fact he does not. This argument turns on Descartes's assumption that, as Matthews puts it later on in the article, he is a 'kind of entity, mind, which is self-transparent; for any act it performs and any state it is in, it cannot doubt that it performs that act or is in that state' (p.133).

ACTIVITY

What is the new concept of mind that Descartes develops, according to Matthews?

DISCUSSION

His ancient and medieval predecessors took the mind to be the rational soul, that is, the capacity for intellection and volition. Descartes's new concept of mind, according to Matthews, is that of consciousness, an indubitable and self-transparent awareness of experience. As Matthews puts it,

> Descartes does something much more than simply isolating one function traditionally assigned to soul, namely, thinking, and supposing it to be independent of the rest. Instead he develops a new concept, consciousness, which includes thinking plus the 'inner part' (so to speak) of sensation and perception.
>
> (Reading 1, p.132)

In short, he replaces rationality with consciousness as the mark of the mental. One of the profound consequences of this is that Descartes in effect redraws the boundaries of the mind that had been set by the Aristotelian and Thomist metaphysical framework that preceded him: he expands the boundaries to include things that were previously considered to be essentially tied to the body. For as Descartes is quick to point out, while he can certainly doubt that he is actually seeing and hearing, since such activities require bodily organs and he can doubt he has a body, since an evil demon may be tricking him into thinking he has one when he does not, he cannot doubt that at least he *seems* to see and hear and taste. The point is vividly driven home by the occurrence of dreams and hallucinations. These 'seemings' to perceive, these sensuous experiences, must be part of his mind, because he cannot doubt that he has them. As Matthews puts it: 'We must "peel off" from seeing, hearing and tasting, etc. the *seeming* to see, hear, taste, etc. which is such that one cannot do that and also doubt that one is doing it. The mind is something that does all and only things of that self-revealing sort' (p.132 below). Thus, where Descartes's predecessors had circumscribed the mental around the intellect and will, Descartes's redefinition of mind as consciousness effectively expands the mental realm so as to encompass the sensuous experience accompanying sensation, perception and imagination. For Aquinas, the immortal rational soul is incapable by itself of any sensuous experiences, imagination or emotion because these are associated only with bodily functions. For Descartes, the immortal and immaterial mind includes sensory experiences – or at least the 'inner' component of sensory experiences – because it includes all and only those things of which one is indubitably aware and one is indubitably aware of putative sensational and perceptual experiences. Philosophers sometimes put this by saying that I can have an experience *as of* a fire without the experience actually being of a fire (I may be hallucinating or dreaming or being deceived by a powerful demon). I can, according to Descartes, have a visual experience as of a fire without any eyes (or even any body at all). As he says in the Third Meditation:

> I am a thing that thinks: that is, a thing that doubts, affirms, denies, understands a few things, is ignorant of many things, is willing, is unwilling, and also which imagines and has sensory perceptions; for as I have noted before, even though the objects of my sensory experience and imagination may have no existence outside me, none the less the modes of thinking which I refer to as cases of sensory perception and imagination, insofar as they are simply modes of thinking, do exist within me – of that I am certain.
>
> (Descartes 1985, vol. II, 24)

For Descartes mind is not rationality but consciousness.

A complication: mind versus the essence of mind

In the above quotation, Descartes very subtly, almost imperceptibly, distinguishes between his acts of intellection and volition, on the one hand, and his sensations and perceptions, on the other. He says he is 'a thing that thinks: that is, a thing that doubts, affirms, denies, understands a few things, is ignorant of many things, is willing, is unwilling, *and also which* imagines and has sensory perceptions' (my emphasis). The fact is that while Descartes thinks that imagination and sensation – at least their 'inner' aspects of which we are necessarily conscious and cannot doubt that we have – belong to mind rather than body, they do not belong to the *essence* of mind, they are not essentially part of what he is. As he makes clear later in the Sixth Meditation:

> I find in myself faculties for certain special modes of thinking, namely imagination and sensory perception. Now I can clearly and distinctly understand myself as a whole without these faculties; but I cannot, conversely, understand these faculties without me, that is, without an intellectual substance to inhere in.
>
> (Descartes 1985, vol. II, 54)

So, for Descartes, the essence of mind, what a mind must necessarily possess if it exists at all, includes only consciousness of acts of intellection and volition. However, minds are also sometimes conscious of other goings-on in them, namely, sensory experiences, but these goings-on are not essential to them, in the sense that a mind could exist without having them (the minds of angels are presumably like this). As we will see presently, the sensings and imaginings that occur in the mind are caused by its attachment to the body. This view raises very serious problems for Descartes.

Descartes's metaphysics: substance, attribute, mode

Descartes is undoubtedly the towering figure in philosophical thought about the mind and his views have profoundly influenced all subsequent philosophical discussion of the nature of mind. This is not to say that all subsequent philosophers have been Cartesians; on the contrary, many of them define themselves as, in one way or another, anti-Cartesian. Indeed, much of twentieth-century philosophy of mind was a reaction to certain Cartesian views, and in fact at the turn of the millennium, though there remains a minority of reactionary Cartesians, the epithet 'Cartesian' is often now used in a pejorative if not abusive fashion. I shall spend the rest of this chapter looking at a notorious problem that receives scant attention by commentators but which in fact reveals vividly the nature of Descartes's dualism: the question whether non-humans animals, according to Descartes, are sentient, capable of sensing and experiencing. The natural view, of course, is that they certainly are. What could be more obvious? The debate over 'animal rights' is not, after all, over whether animals suffer pain but whether their so suffering it at the hands of humans is ever morally permissible. There is no question that they suffer pain. It is not altogether clear whether Descartes can accommodate this. The point of asking the question whether on Descartes's view animals can sense and experience is not simply to answer it for its own sake, interesting as it is; for in seeking an answer to the question, we bring out one of the two most important aspects of Descartes's philosophy of mind: his epistemological take on the mental, his view that what unites all mental phenomena under the heading of 'mental' or 'mind' is that we are aware or conscious of them. The other aspect is his perhaps better-known claim that the mind is an immaterial substance. Together, these two features of Descartes view give rise to serious problems. Before we can see what these problems are, it is necessary to look briefly at Descartes's basic metaphysics.

Descartes is the most famous substance dualist. According to him, with the one exception of God, every thing that exists is either corporeal or incorporeal, that is, either a material substance or a mental substance. Descartes operates with three basic categories of being (ontological categories): substance, attribute and mode. Substances are those things capable of independent existence, and there are exactly two kinds: mind and matter (again excluding the kind of substance God is, for He is the only truly independent existent and on whom mind and matter ultimately both depend). Attributes depend on substances in the sense that they are always properties of substances; they cannot exist apart from any substance. There are two 'principal attributes': extension and thought, the essential or defining properties of matter and mind, respectively. Modes, in turn, depend on attributes in the sense that they are always properties or 'modifications' of attributes, that is, of either extension or thought. Modes, like attributes, are properties of substances, but they are so in particular always as changes in the basic properties of extension or of thought. Each mode is a modification of only one of the principal attributes: either extension or thought but not both. So, for example, being square or being in motion are modes of the attribute extension – they are different ways of being extended – which is in turn the principal characteristic of matter. Likewise, sensing, willing, perceiving and the rest of the mental panoply are modes of thinking, that is, modifications of the attribute of thought which is the essential property of mind. Each of us, during our earthly existence, is a combination of mental and material substances, namely, our mind and our body. Our bodies operate according to mechanical principles that do not differ in kind from the mechanical principles that govern non-living material substances. Descartes sometimes refers to the 'mechanism of our body'. Our minds are a substance in which take place various 'modifications' or changes, which Descartes broadly characterizes as thoughts or thinking. For Descartes the term 'thought' covers an unusually wide range of phenomena. As he says in the *Principles of Philosophy*:

> By the term 'thought', I understand everything which we are aware of as happening within us, insofar as we have awareness of it. Hence, *thinking* is to be identified here not merely with understanding, willing and imagining, but also with sensory awareness. For if I say 'I am seeing, or I am walking, therefore I exist', and take this as applying to vision or walking as bodily activities, then the conclusion is not absolutely certain. This is because, as often happens during sleep, it is possible for me to think I am seeing or walking, though my eyes are closed and I am not moving about; such thoughts might even be possible if I had no body at all. But if I take 'seeing' or 'walking' to apply to the actual sense or awareness of seeing or walking, then the conclusion is quite certain, since it relates to the mind, which alone has the sensation or thought that it is seeing or walking.
>
> (Descartes 1985, vol. I, 195)

Is sensory experience a bodily process or a mental process?

This substance dualism naturally and urgently raises the question of the relation between the body and the mind. After all, I can move my body and my body can produce states of mind within me. It certainly seems that body and mind causally interact with each other. Descartes did not deny this and while he thought that, ultimately, what he famously called the 'union' and 'intermingling' between mind and body was beyond our capacity for understanding, he did say some fairly detailed things about the nature of the processes leading up to the interaction between the two. Setting aside most of Descartes's outdated physiological details, he thought that the location of 'contact' between the mind and body was the pineal gland in the brain. Motions in the pineal gland cause various states of mind and the mind itself can move the pineal gland. When we decide to walk or talk the mind causes the pineal gland to move in a certain way that sets off a chain of movements through the body, via the nerves, blood, and muscles, terminating in our legs moving in a walking fashion or our tongues moving in a talking fashion. Similarly, when various objects and qualities impinge upon our sensory organs, a certain kind of motion is set up throughout the body, which terminates in the movement of the pineal gland that in turn produces sensory awareness in the mind.

In the following passage from Descartes's 'Sixth Set of Replies' to objections to the *Meditations*, Descartes explains that there are three 'grades' of sensory response:

> The first is limited to the immediate stimulation of the bodily organs by external objects; this can consist in nothing but the motion of the particles of the organs and any change of shape and position resulting from this motion. The second grade comprises all the immediate effects produced in the mind as a result of its being united with a bodily organ which is affected in this way; such effects include the perceptions of pain, pleasure, thirst, hunger, colours, sound, taste, smell, and the like, which arise from the union and as it were intermingling of the mind and body, as I explained in the Sixth Meditation. The third grade includes all the judgements about things outside us which we have been accustomed to make from our earliest years.
>
> (Descartes 1985, vol. II, 294–5)

When we look at a stick, for example, Descartes goes on to explain, the first grade of sensory response consists in various motions in the optic nerve and brain. The second grade comprises the perception of colour and light; and the third is the rational judgement that the stick has various properties, such as a certain size and shape. Waiving the outdated physiology, this is a very plausible characterization of the perceptual process of an attentive and properly functioning rational creature.

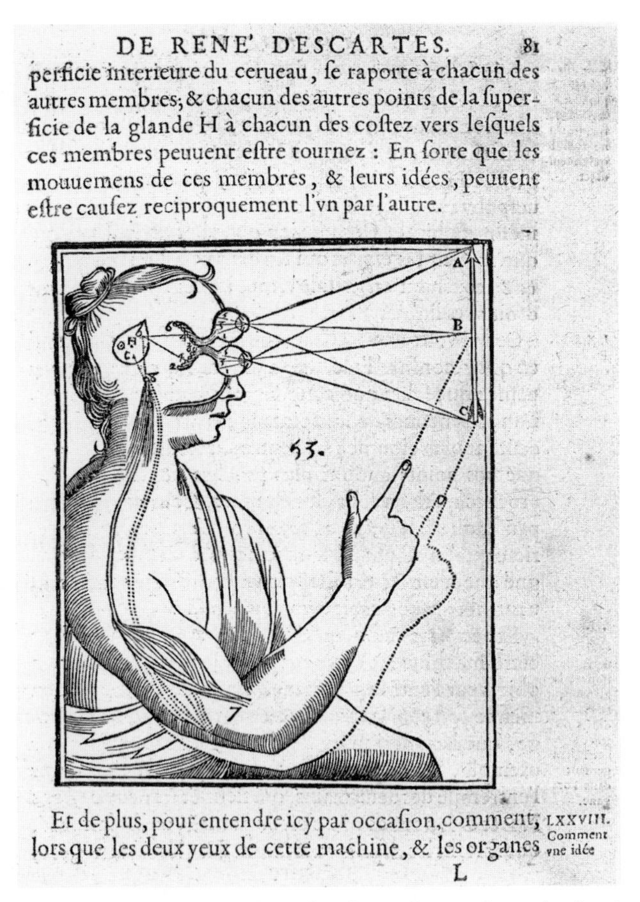

DE RENE' DESCARTES. 81

perficie interieure du cerueau, ſe raporte à chacun des autres membres; & chacun des autres points de la ſuperficie de la glande H à chacun des coſtez vers leſquels ces membres peuuent eſtre tournez : En ſorte que les mouuemens de ces membres, & leurs idées, peuuent eſtre cauſez reciproquement l'vn par l'autre.

Et de plus, pour entendre icy par occaſion, comment, lors que les deux yeux de cette machine, & les organes

LXXVIII. Comment vne idée

L

Figure 1 Descartes: Coordination of muscle and visual mechanisms by means of pineal body. Copyright © Wellcome Library, London.

ACTIVITY

Given Descartes's metaphysical hierarchy of substance, attribute and mode, in which substance – mind or body – do you think each grade of sensory response occurs? Put a tick in the appropriate box.

Grade of sensory response	*Mind*	*Body*
Grade 1: motion, change of shape and position		
Grade 2: perceptions of pain, pleasure, colours, smell, etc. (i.e., 'sensation' – see below)		
Grade 3: judgements		

DISCUSSION

The first grade clearly occurs in body, as it consists of motion and change of shape and position, and all these processes are modes of extension, the principal attribute of body. The third grade clearly occurs in mind, as it involves judgement, which is a mode of thought, the principal attribute of mind. A problem arises, however, when we ask: In which substance – the mind or the body – does the second grade occur? Given Descartes's metaphysical system, the feeling of pain and pleasure (or the 'perception' of these things, as Descartes puts it – a point we shall return to in the next chapter) and the seeing of colour must occur in either the body or the mind – even if they are generated by the 'intermingling' of the two. Let us refer to this second grade of sensory response as 'sensation'. Sensation is a mode, according to Descartes. All modes are modifications of either extension or thought, the two principal attributes, and each and every mode is the modification of only one of these principal attributes. Sensation then is a mode of either extension or thought, but not both. There are, then, two alternatives to consider. Let us take each in turn.

Sensation as a mode of thought

Suppose that sensation is a mode of thought and thus occurs in the mind. If sensation occurs in the mind and animals have sensations (they feel pain, for example), then fairly obviously we can infer that animals have minds. Unfortunately, Descartes denied that animals had minds, and this is evidently not something is he is prepared to give up, implying, as it does for him, that they have immortal souls. This means that if he accepts this alternative, if he treats sensation as a mode of thought, then he must embrace the counter-intuitive implication that animals do not have sensations (for they most definitely do not have minds, according to Descartes). Let us consider the other alternative.

Sensation as a mode of extension

Suppose that he holds that sensation is in fact a mode of extension and thus occurs in the body. He can then maintain both that animals have sensations but that they do not have minds. Dogs can feel pain even though they have no minds because pain is a corporeal process. The problem with this alternative is that is does not appear to be consistent with Descartes's claim that an evil demon could deceive me into thinking that I am sitting before the fire, feeling its heat and seeing its flames, even though I had no body.

Recall that on Descartes's new concept of mind as consciousness, the mind consists of the indubitable awareness it has of everything that goes on in it. Now, I can be aware of its seeming to me *as if* I am seeing and hearing, since I can be having sensual visual and auditory 'as of' experiences. But this would not be possible if the sensations involved in these experiences are bodily occurrences and I had no body. But Descartes insists that I can have such conscious experiences as seeming to see and hear without a body (an evil demon could give me these kinds of hallucinatory experiences, or I could be dreaming, without possessing a body). If this is right, then it follows that sensations are not in fact bodily processes. For, to repeat, if they were bodily processes, then it would not be possible to hallucinate or dream that I am seeing without having a body.

Descartes's dilemma

Descartes, then, seems faced with a dilemma: according to his substance dualism, sensations (the second grade of sensory response, which consists of sensuous experiences as of colours, smells, etc.) are either part of the mind or part of the body (but not both). If sensations are part of the mind, then it follows that animals do not have any (because animals do not have minds). This is extremely counter-intuitive and not something many of us would be prepared to accept. If sensation is part of the body, on the other hand, then, while animals may have sensations because they have bodies, it is wrong to suppose, as Descartes also does, that we could be having them at the same time as being deceived that we had a body when we do not.

A way out of the dilemma? Two senses of 'sensation'

Perhaps, however, we need to reconsider Descartes's third grade of sensory response here: that is, the *thought* or *judgement* that things are thus and so; that, for example, there is a large bronze equestrian statue before me or that I am sitting before a roaring fire. We can also make judgements about our own sensations and perceptions, which for Descartes is simply to say that we are aware of our sensations and perceptions. I can not only see a fire but I can be aware that I see a fire. What if we assign (second-grade) sensation to the body and (third-grade) sense-based judgements to the mind? My body, as it were, has visual experiences and sensations of pain; but it is my mind that is aware of these visual experiences and feelings of pain. On this view, animals can then have sensory experiences – they can feel pain and have visual and auditory sensations – but they cannot have an awareness of these sensory experiences, in the sense that they are incapable of judging that they are having such experiences. This seems right. A dog cannot think to itself, reflecting upon its own visual experience, 'I seem to be having an experience of several rabbits leaping about' or judge that it is having such an experience; it can only have the experience and react accordingly, say, by breaking into chase. And it appears that it can now seem to us that we are having sensory experiences without our having a body. For while the body has the actual sensations, it is the mind that does the judging that the sensations are occurring. It is very tempting to defend Descartes along these lines (cf. Baker and Morris 1996) and to rescue him from the dilemma he faces. The idea is that Descartes distinguished between two senses of 'sensation'. Take 'seeing', for example. There is what we might call *sensuous seeing*, which is the having of visual experiences and which corresponds to the second grade of sensory response. It is essential that sensuous seeing need not be veridical; it can be, but need not be, for it could be produced by dreams or hallucinations. The point is simply that sensuous seeing is the having of putative visual experiences, be they veridical or not. Sensuous seeing is a bodily process. Then there is what we might call *judgemental seeing*, which is the *judgement* or *awareness* that one is sensually seeing and which corresponds to the third grade of sensory response. In judging that one is sensuously seeing one does not know whether one is actually seeing or merely hallucinating or dreaming; what one does know is that putative visual experiences as of colour and light are occurring in one. Judgemental seeing is mental process. Given this distinction, we can then say that animals can sensuously see, because they have bodies, but only humans can judgementally see, because only they have minds; that is, only humans can judge that they are sensuously seeing. On this interpretation, an evil demon cannot of course implant sensuous seeing within me without my having a body (because, by hypothesis, sensuous seeing is bodily). But he can still trick me, for he can give me judgemental seeing, that is, he can make me judge that I am sensuously seeing even when I have no body (because, by hypothesis, judgemental seeing is purely mental). So, on this interpretation, the fact, if it is a fact, that I cannot doubt that I seem to be seeing, is a matter of my not being able to doubt that I am conscious of sensuous experiences occurring within me, that is, of my not being able to doubt that I am judgmentally seeing – because only judgemental seeing is a purely immaterial process.

Unfortunately, this distinction between the judgement or awareness that sensations are occurring – for example, judgemental seeing, the third grade – from the experiential occurrence of the sensations – for example, sensuous seeing, the second grade – does not really help Descartes. The reason is that judgemental seeing entails sensuous seeing. Since, on the third view under discussion, by which we are trying to rescue Descartes from his dilemma, we are assuming for the sake of argument that sensuous seeing entails having a body, it follows that judgemental seeing entails having a body. Why does judgemental seeing entail sensuous seeing? For the simple reason that if I am aware that I am having visual experiences, say, then surely I must actually be having visual experiences (whether veridical or not). It does not make any sense to suppose that I might judge that I am having a visual experience as of a roaring fire, whether it be veridical or hallucinatory, without actually having such an experience. Under the assumption that sensuous sensations are bodily processes, it follows that if I have no body I cannot be undergoing any. Without a body I cannot have any kind of sensuous experience at all. So, if I am to be aware of its seeming to me as if there is a statue or a fire before me, or that I am in pain, this must be a purely intellectual act, a judgement devoid of any sensuous phenomenology (no veridical or hallucinatory awareness of colours or shapes or sounds or heat). Recall the phenomenon of blindsight, discussed in the first chapter, and imagine a creature with a case of 'global' or multi-modal blindsight who is somehow able to make judgements (as opposed to just guesses) about perceptions of colour and light. If I were such a creature I would be in my body 'like a sailor in a ship', inspecting the condition of my ship without actually *experiencing* the condition of my ship – and this is famously precisely how Descartes *denies* we are in our bodies. Recall the letter Descartes wrote, quoted in the first chapter (p.8), in which he says that if an angel were in a human body it would not have any feelings but would simply observe changes in its nervous system and make intellectual judgements about its bodily states. We are not merely attached to our bodies in the manner of an angel who pilots a borrowed body around to carry messages to earth – we are *intermingled* with our bodies and this intermingling explains our possession of what angels lack: sensuous experience. When we seem to be seeing or walking, that is, when we judge we are seeing or walking, we are having sensuous experiences. The reason why I judge that I am seeing a fire is that I am having sensuous experiences as of a fire. And, according to the interpretation of Descartes that we are now considering, I can only have such experiences if I have a body. It follows that it can seem to me that I am seeing a fire only if I have a body; that is, I can judgementally see a fire only if I have a body.

Let us consider this matter in a little more detail. When Descartes is sitting in his room meditating before the fire, he has a variety of visual-, auditory-, tactile- and olfactory-like experiences: he seems to be surrounded by walls and furniture, to be writing on paper with a quill and ink; it is as if he sees flames dancing in the hearth and can hear the fire crack and pop and feel the warmth on his face and the smell of the burning logs. All this could be going on within him, according to Descartes, even though he was disembodied. It is logically possible for all this to be occurring within him even though he has no body. He may be deceived about whether he is actually in a room before a fire but there can be no doubt that it seems to him as if he is and he can judge that it so seems to him. The basis of this judgement, this judgemental seeing, is his sensuous experience, his sensuous seeing, whether it be veridical or hallucinatory. The idea of our being *aware* that we are having visual experiences, or judging indubitably that we are, without actually having any, does not even make sense. What can it mean to judge indubitably that one is in pain without actually being in pain? Or to judge indubitably that one seems to be seeing a fire and feeling warmth without actually having any veridical or hallucinatory sensuous experience at all? There must be some kind of sensuous experience upon which the indubitable judgements in question are based or from which they arise. In short, if it is possible for all this indubitable awareness of sensuous seemings to occur without a body then it cannot be that all sensory experience is a bodily process. There is simply no way of peeling off the conscious *judgemental* side of seeming to see from the *sensuous experience* of seeming to see itself. In the end, then, relegating 'second-grade' sensations, sensuous seeings, to the material body and 'third-grade' judgements, judgemental seeings, to the immaterial mind is once again incompatible with Descartes's view that it can seem to me that I am having sensuous experiences even though I have no body. Alas, we have failed to rescue Descartes from the dilemma.

Descartes's answer: sensory experience is a mental process

My own view is that Descartes boldly impales himself on one of the horns of the dilemma by holding that sensory experience – the second grade – is a mode of thought and hence occurs wholly and only in the mind. He thus thought that animals were incapable of having sensations and hence incapable of feeling pain (because they have no minds). This is borne out to some extent by his remark, in a letter to his friend Mersenne, that:

> I do not explain the feeling of pain without reference to the soul. For in my view pain exists only in the understanding. What I do explain is all the external movements which accompany this feeling in us; in animals it is these movements alone which occur, and not pain in the strict sense...
>
> (Descartes 1985, vol. III, 148)

In another letter written to Mersenne a month later he says: 'As for brute animals, we are so used to believing that they have feelings like us that it is hard to rid ourselves of this opinion' (ibid., 149). One should remember, though, that Descartes expressly denied that he could *prove* that animals had no thought or sensation, since 'the human mind does not reach into their hearts'.

On Descartes's view, then, the body causes, or as he often says 'occasions' or 'produces', sensations in the mind. It is, strictly speaking, the mind that feels but the mind is caused to feel by the motions of the pineal gland in the brain. These motions 'occasion' feelings in the mind. Movements in the pineal gland are not the only possible proximate causes of feelings, of course. God, or a very powerful malicious demon, could also cause a mind to have these feelings even though that mind had no brain or body– though the fact that God is not a deceiver guarantees that this never actually happens.

In the case of vision, the matter in motion in our brains causes, occasions or produces in the mind visual experiences of the scene before our eyes and this occasion is 'ordained by nature'. That is, God has arranged the world in such a way that certain motions of matter lawfully cause certain sorts of sensations in souls. As far as human comprehension is concerned that is an end to it; there is no further explanation of how matter in motion can produce sensations in souls other than that God in His infinite and benevolent wisdom has decreed that it be so for the benefit and welfare of humankind.

A similar view is expressed later by the seventeenth-century English philosopher John Locke (1632–1704). Locke thought that when it comes to the question of how a chunk of matter, *or an immaterial soul*, could have sensory experiences (or thoughts), all that can be said is that God has so arranged things and that it is beyond our powers to understand. Unlike Descartes, however, Locke argued for agnosticism about whether sensations (and thoughts) were properties of material bodies or immaterial souls. He thought that, so far as we can tell, neither position is more tenable than the other and that God could have arranged things either way. If God has taken the former option, then He has seen to it, by an act of 'super addition', that certain chunks of matter, which are organized in certain ways, produce thoughts and sensations. By a divine act of will He has 'superadded' sensations and thoughts to what would otherwise be insensate and unthinking chunks of matter. There is nothing in the essential nature of matter which can give rise to mentality; so, if matter does indeed have mentality, then this is because God has added mentality as an extra feature, as it were, that goes beyond its essential nature. In fact, for Locke, life itself, as well as sensation and thought, must be added by God to matter because there is nothing in inert matter that can, by itself, give rise to life. Matter can no more have vegetative properties than it can have sensitive or rational ones. Thus Locke (writing fifty years after Descartes) is an advocate of the older Aristotelian bifurcation between mechanism and life. In this respect he is less radical than Descartes who sought to collapse this distinction, holding that the difference between the quick and the dead is just like the difference between a clock that is working and one that is broken. Nevertheless, Descartes and Locke agree that whatever substance it is that sensations inhere in, there is no natural explanation for why sensations accompany bodily goings-on; it is God's providence. It seems to follow from this that it is possible for healthy and properly functioning animal bodies to lack sensation altogether. Descartes's view then is that God has ordained that our souls experience tickling sensations and sensations of pain when we undergo certain bodily processes but that this is not true of animals or artificial machines. While the idea that the physiological activities in dogs' nervous systems never give rise to feelings of pain is a very strange and counter-intuitive thesis, it is at least intelligible. We seem to be able to imagine that the yelps and cries of dogs and other animals – indeed, humans too – are not accompanied by the feeling of painfulness. After all, actors often pretend to be in great pain when they are not. But what about the *vision* of dogs? Does it really make sense to deny that dogs see? Descartes does say in the *Optics* that 'it is the soul which sees, and not the eye' (Descartes 1985, vol. I, 172) and 'we know for certain that it is the soul that has sensory awareness, and not the body' (ibid., 164). Moreover, Descartes was well aware that circular objects project oval images onto the retina and so he stresses that the 'pictures' in the brain (which are just certain configurations of matter in motion) do not resemble the objects they are pictures of, and that even if they did, it is not in virtue of any such resemblance that we see things, for that would require, absurdly, that we have eyes in our head in order to see the pictures (ibid., 167). Rather, according to Descartes, the corporeal pictures in the brain occasion the soul's having 'ideas' that do resemble, when things are working properly, external objects. Visual experiences are triggered in the soul by the movements of the pineal gland. Descartes is in part attacking the Aristotelian hylomorphic conception of perception held by the scholastics, according to which to see an apple is for the form of the apple to be transmitted without its original matter, via the eye, to the brain where it is realized in a different way in the matter of the brain. Descartes objects to the scholastic idea that objects send out images of themselves – 'sensible forms' – that travel into our eyes eventually 'informing' the grey matter of our brain. On the contrary, argues Descartes, when we judge that there is a certain object before us,

> We make such a judgement not because these things transmit the ideas to our mind through the sense organs, but because they transmit something which, at exactly that moment, gives the mind occasion to form these ideas by means of the faculty innate to it. Nothing reaches our mind from external objects through the sense organs except certain corporeal motions...but neither the motions themselves nor the figures arising from them are conceived of by us exactly as they occur in the sense organs, as I have explained at length in my *Optics*. Hence it follows that the very ideas of the motions themselves and of the figures are innate in us. The ideas of pain, colours, sounds and the like must be all the more innate if, on the occasion of certain corporeal motions, our mind is to be capable of representing them to itself, for there is no similarity between these ideas and the corporeal motions.
>
> (Ibid., 304)

These 'ideas' of pain and colour and so on, which are triggered by motions in the pineal gland, are produced by a capacity that is *innate* in the mind. This is really a quite extraordinary thesis. Descartes is saying that God has furnished our immaterial minds with a faculty that can produce, all on its own, enough visual experiences to correspond to any external scene before our eyes on any occasion. The idea is that when external objects cause motions in our eyes and brains, these motions occasion the innate faculty to produce a visual experience to occur in a manner that is appropriate to the representing of the objects in question. It follows that creatures without minds do not have an 'innate stock' of visual experiences that are triggered by motions in their eyes. On this view, the 'movements' which compose the retinal images on a dog's eye simply act in a mechanical fashion in a way which causes a dog's legs to move or mouth to bark. The dog does not have a visual experience in the way that we do; it has no 'ideas' of colour and sound. Its visual process terminates with the movements constituting the corporeal picture in its brain that only vaguely resembles the objects of sight. Thus, Descartes's remark in his letter to Henry More, explaining his views on animals, 'I deny sensation to no animal, insofar as it depends on a bodily organ' should, I think, be interpreted in a way in which sensation 'insofar as it depends on a bodily organ' means a purely physiological process akin to the ones Descartes attributes to the 'man-machine' in the passage from *Treatise of Man* quoted by Matthews. Descartes, I believe, is committed to the view that in a very real sense, animals do not see or feel pain, for they have no souls in which occur visual experiences and pains.

Figure 2 Descartes: The path of burning pain. Copyright © Wellcome Library, London.

But how do I know that you who are reading this are enjoying visual experiences or suffering pain rather than simply acting as if you are, all the while lacking any conscious experience, like Descartes seems to view the dog? The possibility that you or I am an automaton seems to follow from Descartes's idea of 'natural ordination' and Locke's 'superaddition'. If God had not superadded the conscious experience of sensations to my body, or if there had been no such natural ordination, then I would have no conscious visual or sensuous experiences. Perhaps, then, all the people around me are automata, animal bodies entirely devoid of any conscious experience. Or perhaps God has arranged things so that in a few *deviant* people the conscious experience that occurs in their minds when they are tickled is acute pain and a ticklish feeling when they hold their hands in the fire. We would never know because their bodily processes and behaviour are exactly like ours. The possibility of automata and deviants, if it is a possibility (Descartes, for one, denied that God created any *human* automata), points to what some contemporary philosophers call the problem of the 'explanatory gap'. It seems that no matter how much we learn about the neurophysiology of the brain, none of it helps us understand how the brain gives rise to conscious experience; there always seems to remain, in the words of Wittgenstein, 'The feeling of an unbridgeable gulf between consciousness and brain-process' (1953, §412, 124). This so-called 'hard problem' of the explanation of consciousness is seen by many to be the most vexing of all problems in the philosophy of mind. Descartes's and Locke's view that bodily processes do not necessarily give rise to conscious experience – that it is possible for there to be physiological processes going on unaccompanied by any conscious experience – is still alive and well in contemporary philosophy of mind, even though the latter has shed the idea that mental processes take place in an immaterial substance. Unlike the ancient, medieval and modern traditions in philosophy, which worried more about the nature of cognition than that of sensation, the situation in contemporary philosophy is almost the reverse: sensation now seems more mysterious than thought. William James pointed out that according to the former traditions in philosophy, 'sensational consciousness is something *quasi*-material, hardly cognitive, which one need not much wonder at. *Relating* consciousness is quite the reverse, and the mystery of it is unspeakable'. But this is wrong, thought James; for him, 'That brains should give rise to a knowing consciousness at all, this is the one mystery which returns, no matter of what sort the consciousness and of what sort the knowledge may be. Sensations... involve the mystery as much as thoughts... involve it' (1983, 647).

Summary

For the Aristotelians, there is a sharp separation between life and mechanism and an intimate connection between life and mentality. What is characteristic of those higher living beings, humans, is their capacity for rationality. It is rationality that sets us apart from all other living creatures. Descartes breaks radically with this view. For him, living beings are simply complicated machines whose workings can be completely explained on the basis of mechanical principles. There is no deep connection between life and mental phenomena; on the contrary, mental phenomena are properties of an immaterial substance, mind, which may be temporarily attached to or, more accurately, 'intermingled' with, a bodily machine. Moreover, for Descartes the mental is not restricted to rationality but is rather simply anything of which we are indubitably aware or conscious, our sensory experiences as well as our acts of intellection and volition. One complication is that for Descartes, the essence of mind is restricted to the consciousness of its acts of intellection and volition, without which it would not exist. While consciousness of sensory experience is not essential to a mind – a mind can exist without it – when a mind is in 'close and intimate union' with a material body, the former has consciousness of sensory experience as well as of rational acts of thought. Descartes's new concept of mind, however, runs into serious trouble with sensory experience. He is forced to say that, although sensory experience is not essential to minds, it is, strictly speaking, a property only of mental substance and thus it only occurs in minds (when they are attached to bodies). Descartes is thus driven to deny that creatures without minds, namely, all non-human animals, have any sensory experience in the way that we humans do. Animals do not have visual experiences in the way that we do and strictly speaking they do not feel pain. They are simply complex machines whose behaviour is completely explicable without reference to any mental phenomena. This view seems to lead to the possibility of automata and deviants. Some of these consequences of Descartes's view may seem to you unacceptable. They certainly did to many philosophers who came after Descartes. In the next chapter we shall leap ahead to the twentieth century and look at one of these philosophers.

Further reading

An excellent introductory text on the change from the medieval conception of the world to the modern one is W.T. Jones's *A History of Western Philosophy Vol III: Hobbes to Hume* (1969), which discusses the rise of modern science and its effects on philosophy. Also very useful is the two-volume *Cambridge History of Seventeenth-century Philosophy*, edited by Daniel Garber and Michael Ayers (1998). Margaret Wilson's posthumously published collection of essays, *Ideas and Mechanism* (1999), discusses many aspects of early modern philosophy. The best current English translation of Descartes's writings is *The Philosophical Writings of Descartes* (3 vols) (1985), edited by John Cottingham, Robert Stoothoff, Dugald Murdoch and Anthony Kenny. *The Cambridge Companion to Descartes* and *Descartes*, both edited by John Cottingham (1992 and 1998), are good collections of essays on Descartes. Cottingham's own *Descartes* (1986) is a very accessible general introduction to Descartes's philosophy. For a slightly more advanced but still accessible introduction to Descartes, see Margaret Wilson's *Descartes* (1978). A brilliant but more difficult book than either of these two is Bernard Williams's justly celebrated *Descartes. The Project of Pure Enquiry* (1978). Two good recent books on Descartes's philosophy of mind in particular are Marleen Rozemond's *Descartes's Dualism* (1998) and Lilli Alanen's *Descartes's Concept of Mind* (2003). There are several good editions of Locke's great work *An Essay Concerning Human Understanding*; both the Oxford (1975) and Penguin (1997) editions, for example. A good short book on Locke is E.J. Lowe's *Locke on Human Understanding* (1995); see Michael Ayers's magisterial *Locke. Epistemology and Ontology* (1991) for a more comprehensive treatment. *Locke*, edited by Vere Chappell (1998) is a collection of essays. Two good places to start on Aristotle's and Aquinas's views on mind are Norman Kretzman's essay on Aquinas's philosophy of mind in *The Cambridge Companion to Aquinas,* edited by Norman Kretzman and Eleonore Stump (1993), and Stephen Everson's essay on Aristotle's psychology, in *The Cambridge Companion to Aristotle*, edited by Jonathan Barnes (1995). *History of the Mind–Body Problem*, edited by Tim Crane and Sarah Patterson (2000), is an excellent collection of recent essays on ancient, medieval, modern and twentieth-century concerns about the mind. John Yolton's *Thinking Matter* (1983) is a scholarly discussion of materialism in eighteenth–century Britain. Susan James discusses the emotions in seventeenth-century philosophy and the general Aristotelian background in her *Passion and Action* (1997). Richard Rorty's take on the rise of modern philosophy in the first chapter of his brilliant but controversial *Philosophy and Mirror of Nature* (1979), 'The invention of the mind', is well worth reading, but should be balanced by Gary Hatfield's critical response 'Epistemology and science in the image of modern philosophy: Rorty on Descartes and Locke' (2001).

CHAPTER 3

From the Inner to the Outer: Ryle's Concept of Mind

In this chapter we will look at one of the most trenchant attacks on the Cartesian concept of mind, that of the Oxford philosopher Gilbert Ryle (1900–76). The attack is presented with great verve in Ryle's stylish and witty book *The Concept of Mind* (first published in 1949), which is one of the great classic works of twentieth-century philosophy. Indeed, so influential and entertaining was Ryle's jargon-free book that some of his ideas made their way into non-philosophical circles. The phrase 'ghost in the machine' is widely used – it is the title of a book by Arthur Koestler and the name of a record by the pop group The Police. Yet the phrase was coined by Ryle in the late 1940s. Ryle's book is both a destructive and constructive work. His destructive aim is to prove that what he calls 'the official doctrine' – a form of Cartesian dualism, although not derived solely from Descartes's theories – is false. In the course of doing so, he will 'rectify' the 'logic of mental-conduct concepts'. Ryle's idea is that Cartesian dualism suffers from an inadequate grasp of concepts of mental phenomena and that this has produced a series of conceptual confusions about the nature of mind. In order to see the mind for what it really is we need a proper grasp of the concepts we use to talk about the mind and mental phenomena. In most of the book Ryle navigates us through what he takes to be the true 'logical geography' of mental concepts, examining in painstaking detail the entire gamut of mental phenomena. In the course of doing so, however, a positive vision of mentality, as Ryle sees it, emerges. I say a 'vision' rather than a doctrine or thesis or position because it is not altogether clear exactly what Ryle's positive view is. He is often labelled a 'behaviourist', someone who thinks that the mind is in some sense really just behaviour, but he himself attacked behaviourism along with Cartesianism.

The ghost in the machine

ACTIVITY

Read the first section of 'Descartes's Myth', Reading 2, pages 136–40.

Ryle refers to what he calls a 'polar opposition between mind and matter'. In fact, he refers to at least five polar oppositions that characterize the mind/matter distinction. What are they?

DISCUSSION

Ryle thinks that there are five pairs of poles that characterize the opposition between mind and matter, according to the 'official doctrine':

matter/consciousness
spatial/non-spatial
public/private
mechanical/non-mechanical
external/internal

Ryle targets the official doctrine as the view that there are two worlds: the physical world and the mental world. The first is composed of matter and the second consists of consciousness. Matter is located in space while the mind or consciousness is not, according to the official doctrine. Since matter is located in space, bodies, which are parcels of matter, can be observed and thus are *public* objects. What happens to my body can, in principle, be witnessed by anyone and hence is no different from the lives of reptiles, trees, crystals and planets. Minds, however, are not in space and thus their workings are not observable by others; their 'careers' are private in the sense that only the mind in question can inspect and monitor what goes on in it. Bodies, being in space, are subject to the mechanical laws that govern all things in space. Minds are not governed by mechanical laws. (Sometimes Ryle says that the official theory holds that the mental realm is 'para-mechanical'.) The last pair of polar terms, internal and external, or inner and outer, is, as Ryle notes, more problematic than the other pairs. Since the mind is not in space it is hard to see how it could be internal. What is it internal to? It cannot be inside the body, nor have things going on inside of it, because it is not located in space. Ryle admits that its adherents intend the inner/outer contrast to be metaphorical but points out that it is common to find lapses into literalness.

Ryle does a good job of drawing out the epistemological consequences of the official doctrine, consequences that were briefly touched on in the previous chapter, when we considered the possibilities of automata and deviants. As Ryle vividly portrays it, according to this view:

> The mind is its own place and in his inner life each of us lives the life of a ghostly Robinson Crusoe. People can see, hear and jolt one another's bodies, but they are irremediably blind and deaf to the workings of one another's minds and inoperative upon them.
>
> (Reading 2, p.138)

Thus the official doctrine of dualism gives rise to the notorious 'problem of other minds': if all you can observe is my body and its behaviour then (a) how can you know what is really going on in my mind; or, even worse, (b) how can you know that I have a mind at all? Perhaps, with reference to the first question, my mind is entirely devoid of conscious experience – perhaps, in other words, I am an automaton, an unfeeling robot. In the third section of 'Descartes's Myth', Ryle describes another possibility:

> for all we can tell, the inner lives of persons who are classed as idiots or lunatics are as rational as those of anyone else. Perhaps only their overt behaviour is disappointing: that is to say, perhaps 'idiots' are not really idiotic, or 'lunatics' lunatic. Perhaps, too, some of those who are classed as sane are really idiots.
>
> (Ibid., p.145)

Since the private, 'inner' world of minds is not accessible to 'external' observers, there is no way of establishing that lunatic behaviour is correlated with true mental lunacy; or that other people's 'pain behaviour' is correlated with painful feelings rather than, say, ticklish feelings. (Recall that Descartes explicitly says it is the soul that feels pain and has ticklish sensations.)

The flip side of this picture, as Ryle notes, and as Matthews draws our attention to, is that each mind has, at least largely, perfect, indubitable knowledge of its own states and processes, a kind of 'privileged access'. Moreover, says Ryle, this privileged access we, and only we, have to the contents of our own minds is a special kind of perception called 'introspection'. A person can, by introspecting, observe (in some non-optical sense) the passing stream of consciousness – all the episodes of his mental life.

This, then, is the official doctrine which Ryle, with 'deliberate abusiveness', calls the 'dogma of the Ghost in the Machine' and which he sets out to demolish. His argument is that the official doctrine is one big mistake: a category mistake.

Category mistakes

ACTIVITY

Read the second section of 'Descartes's Myth', Reading 2, pages 140–3.

What is a category mistake?

DISCUSSION

A category mistake is the mistake of assigning something to a category to which it does not belong or misrepresenting the category to which something belongs. For example, to think that, since we can lose our tempers and lose our wallets, both tempers and wallets belong to the same category of 'things', would be to commit a category mistake. Tempers and wallets do not belong to the same category despite the fact that both of them can be lost. We can commit a category mistake indirectly when we ascribe to something of one category a property attributable only to things of another category. For example, to say that the number two is furious would be to commit a category mistake because the category of things that can be furious does not include numbers.

Obviously no one with even an inkling of what numbers are would utter such an absurd solecism as this last one. But there are examples of statements that, while perfectly sensible, are prone to give rise to category mistakes. Take, for example, 'Her reputation preceded her', 'He did it for the sake of his mother' or (to borrow an example from the Australian philosopher Keith Campbell) 'That guy gave me the creeps'. Although the last statement has a grammatical form similar to 'That guy gave me the diamonds' it would be a mistake to think that some person handed over some objects – 'creeps' – to me in the way in which someone might hand over some diamonds to me. The second statement is grammatically similar to 'He did it for the friend of his mother' but no one supposes that there is some object answering to the description 'the sake of his mother' in the way in which there is an object answering to the description 'the friend of his mother'. Again, while reputations can precede people, they do not do so in the way an object might precede a person ('Her valet preceded her'). Not all nouns or noun phrases pick out entities. To lose one's temper or one's voice is not to lose an entity, an object, like a wallet or a dog.

The Cartesian category mistake

ACTIVITY

Read the final two sections of 'Descartes's Myth', Reading 2, pages 143–8.

What kind of category mistake, exactly, do the advocates of the dogma of the ghost in the machine commit, according to Ryle?

DISCUSSION

Ryle thinks that when it comes to the term 'mind' and other mentalistic terms, there is a tendency, especially among those who speculate and theorize about mentality, to take the concept of mind and related mental concepts to refer to objects or entities when in fact, according to Ryle, they do not. The basic error is thus to treat the mind as a thing, an object or entity, to which things can happen and in which processes and events occur – in short, to reify the mind. Just as Oxford University 'is not another collateral institution', is not an 'extra member of the class of which these other units [the colleges, libraries, museums and so on] are members', so too minds are not extra members of the class of objects that includes bodies. The mind is not an entity additional to the body, and mental phenomena are not things over and above bodily phenomena.

Ryle thinks that Descartes and others, compelled as they were to embrace the new mechanical and mathematical science of nature, pioneered by Galileo and others, rightly saw that the new mechanism was inapplicable to mental phenomena. But they wrongly concluded from this that the mind and mental phenomena generally must be entities and processes of a radically different kind from bodies and bodily processes. As Ryle says,

> The differences between the physical and the mental were thus represented as differences inside the common framework of the categories of 'thing', 'stuff', 'attribute', 'state', 'process', 'change', 'cause and effect'. Minds are things, but different sorts of things from bodies; mental processes are causes and effects, but different sorts of causes and effects from bodily movements. And so on'.
>
> (Ibid., pp.143–4)

One can add: physical processes are mechanical, mental ones 'para-mechanical'. The reification of the mind and mental states and processes is the source of the 'double-life theory'. But, if the mind is not a thing over and above the body (and mental processes are not occurrences additional to bodily processes), then what is it, according to Ryle? Or, rather, since there is no 'it' to which the term 'mind' refers, what makes it true to say that a creature has a mind or mentality?

Ryle's concept of mind

ACTIVITY

Consider Ryle's illustrations of category mistakes. If a person's mind is not an inner arena in which take place events and episodes of a special 'ghostly' nature, then what do Ryle's illustrations suggest he thinks the mind really is?

DISCUSSION

In two words, the suggestion seems to be that for Ryle the mind is *outward behaviour* or the capacity or ability to engage in various kinds of outward behaviour, all of which are public and hence observable by others. As he says in the first sentence of chapter two of *The Concept of Mind*, 'when we describe people as exercising qualities of mind, we are not referring to occult episodes of which their overt acts and utterances are effects; we are referring to those overt acts and utterances themselves' (Ryle 2000, 26). Just as Oxford University consists of the various colleges, libraries and museums and the way they are related to each other, and an army division consists of its battalions, squadrons and batteries and their interrelations, so too the mind is just various bodily activities and the way these bodily activities are related to each other. So, a man who is vain tends to do certain things such as talk about himself and associate with certain kinds of people. To have the belief that it is going to rain is, similarly, to engage in certain kinds of behaviour, such as keeping a coat handy, storing things indoors and so on.

Now, attitudes like belief, desire and fear, and character traits like vanity and pride, are not exactly the behaviour itself, for a person can possess these mental states and yet not engage in any behaviour at all. After all, a person might be completely paralyzed and still believe things and still be a vain person. Rather, as Ryle discusses in detail elsewhere in *The Concept of Mind*, mental states are, he claims, *dispositions* to behave in certain ways. A disposition is a *tendency* to exhibit or manifest something in certain kinds of circumstances; it is not the exhibition itself, for an object can have a certain disposition even if it never manifests it. An aspirin, for example, is soluble in water; it has the property of solubility – though it may never encounter any water in its history and so never actually dissolve. Solubility is a disposition, the disposition to dissolve when placed in water. Similarly, thinks Ryle, for beliefs and desires. For example, he says

> The gardener who... expects rain need not be repeatedly switching his attention from gardening tasks to silent or vocal prognostications of rain; he just leaves the watering-can in the tool-shed, keeps his coat handy, beds out more seedlings, and so on. He anticipates the rain not by delivering occasional or incessant verbal presages, but by gardening appropriately.
>
> (Ibid., 168)

And again:

> Overt intelligent performances are not clues to the workings of minds; they are those workings. Boswell described Johnson's mind when he described how he wrote, talked, ate, fidgeted and fumed'.
>
> (Ibid., 57)

The one difference between solubility and believing is that where solubility is a 'single-track' disposition, that is, it has a single manifestation, beliefs and desires and other mental states are 'multi-track' dispositions, by which he means dispositions that have various different kinds of manifestation, depending on the kind of circumstances in which they are triggered. As he says,

> When Jane Austen wished to show that specific kind of pride which characterized the heroine of *Pride and Prejudice*, she had to represent her actions, words, thoughts, and feelings in a thousand different situations. There is no one standard type of action or reaction such that Jane Austen could say 'My heroine's kind of pride was just the tendency to do this, whenever a situation of that sort arose'.
>
> (Ibid., 44)

Ryle's concept of mind and the problem of other minds

A virtue of Ryle's 'outer' view of the mind is that, insofar as we take him to be endorsing the extreme behaviourist view that there simply is nothing but outward behaviour and dispositions to behave, there is no longer any 'problem of other minds'.

ACTIVITY

Why is this?

DISCUSSION

The mind is entirely public and open to view because mind is behaviour and dispositions to behave, which are outer and thus accessible to others. For Descartes there is only a *contingent* connection between mental states and behaviour, since mental states cause or 'occasion' behaviour. It follows that others must make a very shaky inference from my behaviour to my states of mind that are hypothesized as the causes of my behaviour. That the inference is shaky is shown by the possibility that I might be an automaton or have a deviant mind. But if there is only behaviour and dispositions to behave then there is no 'logical gap' between behaviour and mental states; they are *necessarily* linked because they are one and the same thing. In seeing a person's outer behaviour we are literally seeing their mind in action, rather than inferring to the existence of a non-observable 'inner' mind. The problem of automata and deviants simply vanishes.

Knowing one's own mind

Another problem, however, arises: we know our own minds better than we know the minds of others.

ACTIVITY

Can Ryle explain this fact?

DISCUSSION

It would seem that for Ryle the explanation must be that we know our own behaviour better than the behaviour of others. But while it is certainly true that I know a lot more about my own behaviour than I know about the behaviour of others, it does not seem that this is the right explanation of how it is that I know my own mind better than I know the minds of others. For in the majority of cases, I need not examine my behaviour at all in order to know what mental states I am in. I just know immediately what I am thinking or feeling without any recourse to my behaviour. Ryle seems unable to cope with the asymmetry that exists between how I know about my own mind and how I know about other minds. Descartes can cope with knowledge of one's own mind but has problems about the knowledge of other minds, whereas for Ryle is just the reverse.

Further problems with Ryle's concept of mind: is it all just dispositions?

There are also problems with the idea that a mental state is a behavioural disposition. We shall consider a commonsensical one in this section and then tackle some slightly more 'technical' ones in the next.

ACTIVITY

Think of the various different kinds of mental phenomena that were discussed in Chapter 1, pages 9–15. Do any of them raise problems for a dispositional analysis? In other words, do you think there any mental phenomena for which it is implausible to regard as behavioural dispositions?

DISCUSSION

While Ryle's claim that beliefs, desires and other attitudes are dispositions to outward behaviour is fairly plausible, for many kinds of mental states and activities, it is just obvious that there is something 'going on' in a person, some kind of event, process or episode. Take thinking, for example. Suppose you are sitting perfectly still for several minutes while you think about whether Cartesian dualism is true. Perhaps you are seated like Rodin's *Le Penseur*, chin on hand, elbow on knee, deep in metaphysical contemplation. Surely something is going on in you, which is accessible, at that moment, only to yourself; a private episode of thinking is occurring. It has a duration that could be timed by a stopwatch. It is very hard to accept that this 'thinking' is no more than your possession of a behavioural disposition to do certain things in certain circumstances, such as report on your 'findings' or yawn. Thinking involves an experiential element and hence involves an occurrence. It cannot be accounted for purely dispositionally (recall the distinction between *dispositions* and *occurrences* in Chapter 1, pp.15–16). In his later writing Ryle struggled with the problem of what *Le Penseur* is doing but arrived at no satisfactory answer (see Lyons 2001, 72–7 for a brief discussion).

Thinking, of course, is not the only kind of mental occurrence. Sensations and perceptions appear to be a species of occurrence and so it is hard to see how they could be accounted for entirely in terms of dispositions to behave. While it is true that I usually behave a certain way when I am in pain, for example, I need not. I might have been poisoned with curare, a substance that can completely paralyze subjects while leaving them fully conscious. Similarly, seeing does not seem to be a pure disposition to behave in certain ways, although it is certainly true that creatures that see do generally behave in distinctive ways. Seeing also involves the occurrence of a visual experience.

Though it is rarely remarked upon by blinkered commentators intent solely on attacking Ryle's alleged behaviourism, the fact is that Ryle does not deny that sensations are occurrences and does not attempt to give behavioural analyses of them. Although at one point, in an Aristotelian or Thomist moment, he says sensations are not mental, strictly speaking, because we share them with the animals, he does not go so far as to deny their existence or to claim that they are nothing but behavioural dispositions. What he does do is attack the idea that sensations are *objects* that are *perceived* and *observed* by the mind. His point is that we do not observe or inspect our sensations, in the way that we observe or inspect a new species of insect; rather, we *have* sensations. Feeling a pain in one's hand is not like feeling a book or a coin in one's hand; to feel pain is just to have pain or be in pain. It is a category mistake to think of sensations as literally objects that can be inspected by the mind.

Suppose that Ryle is right that we do not observe and inspect our own sensations. What is the force of this? Well, it might be a blow to one element in Descartes's view of the mind, for Descartes often speaks as if we do inspect the contents of our minds, as if sensations and experiences were objects in a passing stream of consciousness that flows by our inner mental eye, in the way that flotsam and jetsam flow by in a river we are looking at. In fairness, however, it must be pointed out that it is not at all clear that Descartes thought that we literally perceived our own sensations, even though he often speaks of perceiving 'ideas' of pain and colour (cf. the quotation from Descartes on page 38). After all, it is questionable whether Descartes's metaphysical scheme of substance, attribute and mode, even allows for sensations to be objects, in the sense of individual particular *entities*.

ACTIVITY

Why is this questionable?

DISCUSSION

For Descartes, sensations are *modes*, that is, modifications of the attribute of thought. Thus they are not objects but changes or alterations in the substance of mind.

At any rate, even if Descartes did hold a kind of 'spectator theory' of sensation, refuting the spectator theory is not enough to show that sensations and experiences are not private mental processes or episodes that we undergo, nor even that they are not a kind of immaterial process.

Another problem with Ryle's concept of mind: behaviour

A more technical objection is that it is just not true that there is a behavioural disposition, or even several, associated with each mental state taken on its own. Consider Ryle's example of the belief that it will rain.

ACTIVITY

If Arch is about to leave the house and he thinks it is going to rain, what kind of behaviour is he likely to exhibit? If Arch believes it is going to rain and has left various possessions outside that would be ruined if it rained, what do you think he will do?

DISCUSSION

At first sight, you might think: making preparations to avoid getting wet, such as carrying an umbrella or wearing a waterproof jacket, or perhaps ensuring that various possessions do not get wet, for example, taking the laptop computer in from the garden.

ACTIVITY

If you had given this kind of answer, what crucial assumptions would you be making about Arch?

DISCUSSION

You would have been assuming that Arch does not want to get wet or that he does not want his computer to get wet. But perhaps he does want to get wet and perhaps he wants, for some reason, to ruin his laptop (he's engaged in an insurance scam, say).

As the British philosopher Peter Geach (b.1916) has pointed out, in response to Ryle's dispositional analysis of the gardener's belief that it will rain,

> When Dr Johnson did penance in Uttoxeter market-place, he may have begun by standing around bare-headed until the threatened shower should fall; this would

> not be recognizable as rain-expecting behaviour without a knowledge of Johnson's wish to do penance.
>
> (Geach 1957, 8)

Geach's point is that having the disposition to make preparations to stay dry is something agents do when they believe it will rain only if they *wish*, unlike Dr Johnson, to stay dry. But Ryle cannot appeal to the mental state of wanting, wishing, or desiring to stay dry because his project seems precisely to analyze mental states in terms of behavioural dispositions. That dispositional analysis will not have advanced any if in the end it must smuggle in through the back door other mental states – for that is just where we started in the first place.

This raises a puzzle which goes to very heart of Ryle's project and takes us back to a point about the interpretation of Ryle I made at the outset: namely, it is not clear to what extent Ryle really is a behaviourist *at all*. The problem is not so much that there is a hidden circularity in his dispositional analyses of mental states – the gardener's behaviour only counts as rain-expecting behaviour if he *desires* not to get wet – but that Ryle makes *no effort whatsoever* to rid his analyses of mentalistic vocabulary. Consider: part of his analysis of vanity is the propensity for the vain person to engage in 'roseate daydreams' and suffer 'sinking feelings' when eminent people forget his or her name. Ryle also says that a person believes that the ice is thin 'if he keeps to the edge of the pond, calls his children away from the middle, keeps his eye on the life-belts or continually speculates what would happen if the ice broke'. Ryle's 'behaviour' is never brute bodily motion and trajectory or 'motor response'. He never says that a person who believes the ice is thin will move their body and limbs in a certain fashion, or will have certain muscle contractions, or engage in certain musculo-skeletal activities. On the contrary: his outward behaviour is inevitably a mentally loaded form of human *action*: looking, speculating, calling, day-dreaming. Ryle clearly has no interest in offering definitions of mental states in terms couched entirely in non-mental vocabulary. There is nothing wrong with this *per se* but it does leave it mysterious just what Ryle's view of the mind and mentality is. Mind is not an inner arena made out of immaterial stuff; but neither is it purely material bodily movements ('motor responses'), such as muscle flexings and limb flailings. Ryle's behaviour is soaked in mentality; it is not 'motions and noises' but rather wavings and callings. But where does this mentality come from? What makes Dr Johnson's waiting for rain a *waiting* rather than simply the movements or non-movements of a particular parcel of flesh and bone? How is Johnson's waiting different from the 'waiting' of a marionette?

A final problem for Ryle's concept of mind: mental causation

One natural answer to this question is that Johnson's behaviour counts as a waiting for rain because it was *caused* by the mental states of *wanting* to get wet and *believing* that the best way to get a good soaking would be to stand around bareheaded in the market place. Johnson's waiting is a waiting, in short, because it has an aetiology that traces back to mental states; in other words, waitings have *mental causes*. But, of course, Ryle does not want to say this because he thinks that mental states are precisely *not* inner causes of behaviour; they *are* the behaviour. For him, 'inner mental causes' smacks of an inaccessible ghostly realm of occult forces.

Ryle does, however, think that behaviour in his sense is caused – it is just that he does not think it has *mental* causes. The causes of behaviour for Ryle are simply various goings-on external to our bodies. So, for example, Ryle says that the cause of a person's passing the salt to his neighbour is his neighbour's asking for it or scanning the table for it. Ryle's idea is that a desire to pass the salt is a disposition to pass the salt in certain circumstances, such as being asked for it. These circumstances cause or trigger the manifestation of the disposition in the same way that striking a fragile object causes it to shatter. The desire is analogous to the fragility and the neighbour's scanning the table is analogous to the striking. The problem with this analogy is that if it is carried all the way it threatens to bring the dreaded mental causes back into the picture. For consider that a certain object's fragility is owed to its internal constitution, namely, its molecular configuration. Fragile and malleable objects have different internal structures that explain their different dispositions. Similarly for the solubility of an aspirin: there is something about its molecular structure that is responsible for its dissolving in water. Fragility, malleability, and solubility are not simply brute facts about objects magically attached or 'superadded' to them. The point is sometimes put, generally, by saying that dispositions have *categorical bases*: there is some actual state of the object that explains its possession of the disposition. So when striking the glass causes it to break there is an intervening state – the molecular structure of the glass – which is part of that causal story. The state of the object plays a causal role in bringing about the manifestation of the disposition. Likewise, when my neighbour asks me to pass the salt, there is something about me that is responsible for my manifestation of the disposition to pass the salt; and that thing is, inter alia, my standing desire to pass the salt to whomever needs it. Ryle leaves out this intermediary step and thus fails to appreciate how difficult it is to do away with inner mental causes. But in forsaking inner mental causes he prohibits himself from the most natural way of explaining why it is that certain bodily movements count as 'behaviour' or 'action' rather than the mere 'motions and noises' of a marionette.

Another problem for Ryle is that, even if we grant him his account of the causation of behaviour – external events trigger behavioural dispositions – it is hard to see how he can accommodate the evident fact that one mental event may cause another mental event. Thinking about bears may cause me to think about how my trapper grandfather had to shoot the bears that came into his log cabin looking for food. In other words, one thought leads to another. But Ryle seems ill-equipped to explain the kind of mental-to-mental causation that occurs in thinking, for there need not be, and very often is not, any intervening external circumstance to trigger any behavioural disposition. Indeed, much of our chains of thinking probably never issue in any form of behaviour at all.

Ryle's mistake is to throw the causal baby out with the ghostly bath water (though at least it is not a category mistake!). He commits his mistake because he is in the grip of a false dilemma: either immaterial 'occult' causes or outward behaviour. There is clearly a third option: inner material causes. That is to say, perhaps mental states are inner causes of behaviour that are identical with internal bodily processes, such as brain processes. We shall see in the next chapter that this is the proposal of materialism about the mind.

Behaviour and behaviourism

In our discussion of Ryle we wondered whether behaviour should be described using mental concepts or without using mental concepts. Ryle's mentally loaded descriptions led to problems. So perhaps we should restrict our descriptions of behaviour to those that do not contain any mental vocabulary, to 'motions and noises', as Ryle would have said. This is the programme referred to as 'logical behaviourism' (also called 'analytical' or 'philosophical behaviourism') and is associated with the logical positivists, especially Carl Hempel (1905–97) and Rudolf Carnap (1891–1970). For complex reasons having to do with the project of the 'unification of science', which we need not enter into here, the logical positivists wished to reduce the science of psychology to that of physics. They saw the first step in this reductionist programme as that of providing analyses or definitions of mental terms using non-mental terms. In other words, they proposed to translate statements about mentality into statements about physical behaviour construed as 'motions and noises'.

But what kind of motions and noises will a person emit when, for example, he or she wants to go down to the market place? A person could walk, skip, run, take the bus, drive or skateboard – and hum or sing or talk or chew gum while doing it. All these different ways of getting to the market place involve myriad different motions and noises, of the legs, arms and tongue. How plausible is it that a behavioural translation of 'wants to go to the market' could fix on motions and noises exhibited by all who want to go to the market place? It is not at all plausible, because there are no pure motions and noises that all such wanters exhibit. The search for motions and noises common to all such people is utterly futile. Some walk, some run, some skip and some jump; some do it slowly, some quickly, some stylishly and some awkwardly; some use a cane, some have only one leg and some have prosthetic limbs. In order to achieve a description with the requisite generality to capture all those who want to go to the market place we need to rise to the level of mental vocabulary, such as 'will endeavour to transport him or herself to the market place', for it is only at that level that they have anything in common. But this is precisely to fail to describe behaviour in purely physical terms. Ryle's analyses owe what plausibility they have – and they have a great deal of plausibility – to his promiscuous employment of mental vocabulary. The logical positivists' analyses suffer from the opposite problem: they are closer to being purely non-mental but at the same time incredibly far from the truth.

Summary

Ryle seems to want to replace Descartes's 'inner' view of the mind with an 'outer' view. According to Ryle, Descartes's view that the mind is an immaterial substance attached to a body – a 'ghost in a machine' – is a category mistake. The mind is not a thing additional to the body and mental states are not inner episodes and occurrences that happen in or to this additional thing, running in parallel to bodily activities that accompany them. Rather, for Ryle, the mind is that bodily activity; more accurately, mental states are dispositions to engage in bodily activity. Unlike Descartes's view, Ryle's account of the mind does not suffer from the problem of other minds. But it has its own problems: first, it seems unable to account for knowledge of one's own mind; second, the view of mental states as dispositions to behaviour does not fit the experiential side of the mental very well, such as sensations and thinking; third, there is no behaviour associated with any given mental state on its own, even in a specified circumstance; fourth, Ryle cannot account for the kind of mental causation that occurs between purely mental events, nor even very satisfactorily for the mental causation of behaviour. Overall, Ryle's positive view of the mind is rather hard to pin down and it is not entirely clear how to interpret his emphasis on the 'outer'.

Further reading

There are many editions of Ryle's *The Concept of Mind.* The recent Penguin edition (2000) is worth getting because it has an introduction by the contemporary philosopher of mind Daniel Dennett, who was a student of Ryle. Ryle's thoughts on thinking can be found in his *On Thinking* (1979). Dennett has woven together a sophisticated form of Rylean quasi-behaviourism and functionalism in his *Brainstorms* (1978) and *The Intentional Stance* (1987), which are essential reading for any student of contemporary philosophy of mind, as is his hugely entertaining but highly controversial *Consciousness Explained* (1991). Jerry Fodor attacks Ryle from a cognitivist perspective in his *Psychological Explanation* (1968) and in the introduction to *The Language of Thought* (1975). Dennett responds in 'A cure for the common cold', reprinted in *Brainstorms*. The first edition of Lycan's reader *Mind and Cognition* (1990) contains two behaviourist writings: one by the psychologist J.B. Watson and another by the logical empiricist Rudolf Carnap. Carl Hempel, another logical empiricist, offers a behaviourist treatment of the mental in 'The logical analysis of psychology', reprinted in *Readings in Philosophy of Psychology*, vol. 1, edited by Ned Block (1980). Two recent reactionary defences of a Cartesian-like 'inner' view of mentality, strongly opposed to any form of behaviourism no matter how weak, are John

Searle's *The Rediscovery of the Mind* (Searle 1992) and Galen Strawson's *Mental Reality* (1994). Anyone interested in the 'inner' and 'outer' aspects of mind will want eventually to read Ludwig Wittgenstein's difficult masterpiece *Philosophical Investigations* (1953). Malcolm Budd's short *Wittgenstein's Philosophy of Psychology* (1989) is a useful secondary source. For a more accessible Wittgensteinian perspective on the mind, see Norman Malcolm's essay 'Consciousness and causality' in D.M. Armstrong and Norman Malcolm, *Consciousness and Causality* (1984).

CHAPTER 4

Synthesizing Inner and Outer: Materialism and Functionalism

> Nor, logically, do we exclude man, as even Descartes did: our knowledge of man today is real knowledge precisely to the extent that it is knowledge of him as a machine.
>
> (Nietzsche, *The Anti-Christ*, §14)

What emerged from the last chapter was that while Ryle appears to view the mind as largely a set of complex behavioural dispositions, he does not seem to view it entirely in that fashion. While he tries to persuade us that a correct account of the 'logical geography' of a large number of mental concepts shows that they do not apply to hidden inner episodes of mentation lurking behind, or running in parallel to, outward behaviour but rather apply to the behaviour itself, or the dispositions so to behave, he does not come straight out and say this about all mental concepts. For example, he does not deny the existence of mental occurrences such as sensations. At the end of the day, it is not entirely clear what remains, for Ryle, of the experiential and phenomenological side of mentality. While Ryle may well be right that it is a category mistake to put sensations into the category of objects that are observed and perceived, even he admits that they can be 'noticed', 'heeded' and 'attended to'. But what then are these things to which we can pay heed, which, properly speaking, we do not perceive or observe but merely *have*? If Ryle believes he has exorcized the ghost from the machine, then are our sensations – our tweaks, tingles and tickles, our glimpses and whiffs, as Ryle derisively refers to them – simply states and processes of the remaining machine? No clear answer emerges from Ryle. The possibility remains, however, that the phenomenological dimension of sensations and experiences, their 'felt qualities', their 'what it is like' aspect, are properties of the bodily machine. Moreover, despite Ryle's denial of inner mental causes, there are good reasons for thinking that dispositions to outward behaviour have categorical bases in the bodily machine.

In the first part of this chapter we shall look at a theory of mind that holds that all mental phenomena are states of the body. This is *materialism* or *physicalism* about the mind and one of its foremost proponents and strongest defenders is the Australian philosopher David Armstrong (b. 1926). In the second part, we will look briefly at the theory of mind known as *functionalism*. Many materialists are attracted to functionalism as a way of overcoming the shortcomings of a view like Armstrong's. As we shall see, one could be a functionalist without being a materialist but few adopt this position. It is more usual to combine functionalism with materialism. In the final chapter, we will look closely at a form of functionalism that takes its inspiration from the computer.

The place of behaviour in our concept of mind

ACTIVITY

Read David Armstrong's article 'The nature of mind', Reading 3.

What truth does Armstrong claim to find in Ryle's behaviourism?

DISCUSSION

The truth Armstrong claims to find in behaviourism is that individual mental states are logically tied to behaviour, not in the sense of being *identical* with behaviour or dispositions to behave, but in the sense that mental states are essentially *causes* of behaviour. It is, according to Armstrong, part of the concept of a mental state – part of what we *mean* by 'the mind' and 'the mental' and 'belief', 'desire', 'pain', etc. – that it is a cause of behaviour.

Notice that this is different from how Cartesianism thinks of the connections between mind and behaviour. For Descartes, the connection between mind and behaviour is contingent. The definition of mentality is consciousness and this kind of activity is completely self-sufficient and utterly independent of any body or bodily behaviour. Conscious mental states and events do indeed cause behaviour, but they need not. They only do so when the mind is in union with the body during our earthly existence. Their essence is not to cause or be caused by behaviour and they could exist even if they never entered into any causal relations with anything physical. Presumably on Descartes's view, the minds of angels, or at least some of them, are precisely like this. For Armstrong, however, it is not merely a contingent fact that mental states cause behaviour, it is part of their very nature to do so, mental states are necessarily connected to behaviour. Just as a fossil, in order to be a fossil, must have been caused by a once-living organism or traces of one, and a poison, in order to be a poison, must cause organisms to become sick or die, so too a mental state is essentially a cause of behaviour. Just as the only kind of rock formations that get called 'fossils' are those caused by once-living organisms, and the only substances that cause organisms to become sick or die are called 'poisons', so too the only kinds of things that get called 'mental states' are those things that are causes of behaviour.

The identity theory

ACTIVITY

1 How does Armstrong define the mental?

2 How does this fit in with a materialist view of the mind?

DISCUSSION

1 Armstrong defines a mental state as 'a state of the person apt for producing certain ranges of behaviour'.

2 This definition connects up with materialism or physicalism in the following way. Science has discovered that the states of people that cause their behaviour are in fact states of the central nervous system. These states might have been states of an immaterial substance or another type of thing. But in fact they are not; the causes of behaviour are purely physical events in the central nervous system.

An analogy might help. A gene is by definition a state of an organism that is responsible for passing on heritable characteristics. Science has discovered that what is responsible for passing on heritable characteristics is the DNA molecule. So a gene is a DNA molecule. A gene might have been another kind of molecule or something altogether different; but, as it happens, it is not, it is the DNA molecule. Similarly, states of the central nervous system are the causes of behaviour; and since mental states and events are, by definition, causes of behaviour, they must be states and events of the central nervous system.

This position is called 'central state materialism' because it identifies mental states with physico-chemical states of the central nervous system. It is also sometimes called the 'type identity theory', because it identifies types of mental states with types of physical states.

Types and tokens

Types are *kinds* of things and tokens are *instances* or *occurrences* of types. Consider the first line of William Blake's poem 'The Tyger'. How many words are there in the first line?

> Tyger! Tyger! burning bright

There are four word tokens and three word types, because there are two tokens of one of the three types ('Tyger').

Alexander the Great's horse, Bucephalus, and Black Beauty are tokens – individual instances – of the type *horse*. My copy of *Middlemarch* and your copy of *Middlemarch* are two different tokens of the same type of novel, George Eliot's masterpiece. The type/token distinction is an extremely useful one that has many applications in ordinary life. For example, it can help resolve ambiguities. Suppose I say to a friend that I saw three reptiles on the heath today. I may mean three different kinds of reptile – two *slowworms*, one *adder* and three *sand lizards*, for example – or I may mean three different individual reptiles, for example, *two adders* and *one slowworm*. In the former case, 'three reptiles' refers to three types of reptile; in the latter, to three token reptiles. Similarly, my headache and your headache are two different tokens of the mental type *headache*; and my belief that Duke Ellington was a jazz composer and your belief that Duke Ellington was a jazz composer are two different tokens of the mental type *belief that Duke Ellington was a jazz composer*.

According to the type identity theory, the mental type *pain* is identical with (is one and the same thing as) a certain physical type, just as the type of liquid *water* is identical with (is one and the same thing as) the physico-chemical type H_2O. What this means is that every token of the type pain – my pain, your pain, Dorothea's pain, Duke's pain and so on – is a token of *the same physical type*. So if the mental type pain is identical with the physical type *c-fibre stimulation* (a certain kind of neural activity) then *all* tokens of pain are tokens of c-fibre stimulation. When you, Duke, Dorothea and I are all in pain, each of our token pains is identical with a token c-fibre stimulation occurring within each of us (a different token in each case, of course), just as each sample of pure water in the universe is identical with a sample of H_2O. The type identity theory thus takes its inspiration from the theoretical identifications of natural science. Chemistry has discovered what water really is: H_2O; molecular biology has discovered what genes really are: DNA molecules. Similarly, advocates of the type identity theory conjecture that neurophysiologists will discover what pain really is: a neural state of excitation in the brain. On Armstrong's view, they will discover what pain really is by discovering what really causes 'pain behaviour'. Since pain is by definition that which causes pain behaviour, according to Armstrong, it follows that if a certain neural state of excitation causes pain behaviour, then pain must be that very neural state.

There is a weaker form of the identity theory, called the 'token identity theory', which says merely that each token mental state or event is identical with a token physical state or event. On this view, it does not follow that my token pain and your token pain are tokens of the same physical type. In other words, while my token pain is identical with a token physical state and so too is your pain, these token physical states in each of us could be *different types* of physical states: pain in me might be *m-fibre stimulation* and pain in you might be *y-fibre stimulation*. Both our pains are indeed physical states or events – and so token identity is a form of materialism – but they are each different kinds of physical states. On this view, it does not follow that *all* pain is a single type of physical state, and so advocates of the token identity theory do not think that the theoretical identifications of natural science are a good model for the relation between the mental and the physical, since these identifications are type identifications. We will return to the reason why some philosophers prefer the token identity theory to the type identity theory.

ACTIVITY

Armstrong's type identity theory proceeds in two stages: a conceptual stage, which involves analysis, and an empirical stage, which involves science. Explain what these stages are.

DISCUSSION

The first stage involves a conceptual analysis of mental concepts. Here we find out a priori (independently of experience) that mental states are states apt for causing behaviour. In the second stage, science discovers a posteriori (that is, through empirical investigation) that these mental causes of behaviour are in fact physical states and processes.

The theory is also sometimes called the 'causal theory' because of the first stage. Armstrong's identity theory (aka the causal theory or central state materialism) is a kind of *naturalism*. Naturalism is the view that all the phenomena in the world can be explained by natural science; there is nothing 'supernatural' that is beyond the scope of scientific explanation. In particular, the mind, just as much as the body, is part of the natural world and hence subject to investigation by the natural sciences that take the features of the natural world as their objects of study. Descartes, of course, is an anti-naturalist about the mind, for he thinks that immaterial souls and their modifications fall outside the scope of scientific (which for him meant mechanistic) explanation. (Unlike Locke, however, he is a naturalist with respect to life, since he seeks to do away with 'vital forces' and the 'vegetative soul', holding that life can be completely explained naturally by mechanism.)

Three problems for Armstrong's type identity theory

The first problem – the painfulness of pain

Is the causation of pain behaviour all there is to pain? It would seem not. Surely there is also the felt quality of painfulness. Armstrong's identity theory seems unable to capture this aspect of pain. This suggests that his claim that a mental state can be defined as a state apt for causing certain sorts of behaviour is inadequate, for it leaves out the painfulness of pain. Moreover, if the supposition of automata is coherent, then it is possible for there to be a creature who is a physical duplicate of me, and hence whose internal states cause the same behaviour as mine, but who feels no pain when he puts his hand in the fire. There seems to be a range of mental states – namely, those with an experiential element, such as pain – whose nature is not exhausted by their causal role in producing behaviour; they involve some kind of experiential quality which at least appears to be logically independent of the causal relations pain states bear to behaviour. Nevertheless, it may well be true that a significant portion of mental states – for example, pure attitude states like belief – are defined by their causal role in the production of behaviour. Moreover, there seems no denying that while the mental state of pain has a felt quality, a phenomenological dimension, it also seems to have a causal role in behaviour. Pain, after all, is normally caused by tissue damage and causes wincing, groaning, screaming and other sorts of pain behaviour. So while

Armstrong's analysis does not *exhaust* the concept of pain, perhaps it captures a lot of it.

The second problem – why the causation of behaviour?

Or does it? One might also question whether all mental states, or even any mental states, are essentially states apt for causing behaviour. Descartes certainly would have rejected this claim and so too do some contemporary philosophers (see, for example, chapter nine of Strawson 1994). Nevertheless, it is very likely that Descartes would have accepted the claim that mental states essentially cause other mental states, as happens during acts of thinking, such as wondering, considering or deducing, or at least that they often follow one another in an ordered succession. Modifications of the immaterial substance of mind can consist of mental processes, chains of purely mental events. So perhaps Armstrong's analysis is correct insofar as it maintains that mental states are states necessarily apt for being *causes* (and effects) but not that they are necessarily apt for being causes of *behaviour* (Strawson 1994).

The third problem: multiple realizability

Armstrong's theory says that pain is identical with (say) c-fibre stimulation, that pain just is c-fibre stimulation. But what if it turns out that no other animals have c-fibres? It would appear that we would have to say no other animals feel pain – let alone any extra-terrestrial or non-organic life-forms that also have no c-fibres. In fact, things seem even worse than this. For how likely is it that everyone who believes that Elvis was the King has one and the same type of brain configuration, e-fibres, say? Not very. Science may discover that there are no types of brain states shared by everything in a given type of mental state, in the way that science did discovered that, contrary to what was once believed, jade is not a single mineral kind, but rather comprises two distinct minerals with different molecular structures: jadeite and nephrite. Connected with this is the problem discussed in the last section of the last chapter about how to describe behaviour. Armstrong's theory faces a similar problem. The behaviour of octopuses, for example, is so very different from that of humans that it is very unlikely that both species of animal share a type of physical state with which one could identify pain or any other kind of mental state. This is because it is very unlikely that each species shares a common kind of physical state that is apt for causing both limb movements and tentacle movements. Nevertheless, presumably (*pace* Descartes) octopuses feel pain. Moreover, is it not at least conceivable that machines and extraterrestrial life-forms might have mental lives of some sort, even though they have no brain states with which to identity their mental states? This has come to be called the objection from 'multiple realizability' because it hypothesizes that mental states might be realized or embodied in diverse creatures in multiply different ways.

Functionalism

It is partly these kinds of considerations that led to the birth of a new theory of mind, which is the current reigning orthodoxy in contemporary analytical philosophy: *functionalism*. The inability of the type identity theory to allow for Martian and machine mentality is not the only reason for its rise. Functionalism takes much of its inspiration from various new fields of study, especially the computer science and cybernetics that arose in Britain and the United States during the Second World War.

Thus, Jerry Fodor, whose views we will examine in the final chapter, wrote in an article in *Scientific American* in 1981:

> In the past 15 years a philosophy of mind called functionalism that is neither dualist nor materialist has emerged from philosophical reflection on developments in artificial intelligence, computational theory, linguistics, cybernetics and psychology. All these fields, which are collectively known as the cognitive sciences, have in common a certain level of abstraction and a concern with systems that process information. Functionalism, which seeks to provide a philosophical account of this level of abstraction, recognizes the possibility that systems as diverse as human beings, calculating machines and disembodied spirits could all have mental states. In the functionalist view the psychology of a system depends not on the stuff it is made of (living cells, mental or spiritual energy) but on how the stuff is put together.
>
> (Fodor 1981, 114)

As Fodor notes, since functionalism views phenomena at a certain level of abstraction from the actual stuff they are made out of, it permits a wide range of things to have minds or mental states, such as machines and even disembodied souls or spirits, as long as the stuff out of which these things are made is organized in the right way. We have seen that, for the behaviourist, mental states or properties are bits of behaviour or dispositions to behave. Just as the solubility of an aspirin is not an entity distinct from the aspirin, but rather a property of the aspirin which disposes it to dissolve in water, so too the mind of a person is just a collection or system of properties possessed by a person that disposes him or her to behave in certain ways. Again, though materialism is often described as the doctrine that the mind is the body or the brain, or the brain and central nervous system, it is better expressed by saying that mental states, events, properties and processes are neurophysiological states, events, properties and processes. Similarly, functionalists usually eschew talk of the mind in favour of talk of mental states and properties. 'The mind' is merely a figure of speech for a system of mental states. Moreover, for the functionalist, the essence of a mental state is not consciousness (*à la* Descartes) or behaviour (*à la* behaviourism) or neural activity (*à la* the type identity theory), but rather the *role* or the *function* that the mental state plays in the overall life of a creature. The essence of the mental is not the kind of stuff it is made of but the 'functional role' it plays in the cognitive system of an individual.

Some analogies should help with this idea. There are many kinds of things which are what they are not in virtue of what they are made out of, but in virtue of what their functions are. Consider clocks. A clock is essentially something that tells the time; but it does not have to be made out of a particular kind of stuff to be able to tell the time. Sundials, grandfather clocks, analogue watches and liquid quartz digital watches are all very different from one another in that they are constructed out of diverse types of materials: metal, rock, wood, plastic, etc. Similarly, consider mousetraps and carburettors, common illustrations of functional kinds. The former are essentially mouse-catching devices; the latter devices for mixing fuel and air. These artefacts are defined by their function, what they do – catching mice, mixing air and fuel – not by what material they are made from. Not only artefacts but biological kinds too are often defined by their function: hearts pump blood and kidneys filter the blood.

Mental states too, according to functionalism, are defined by their function. In other words, what makes a mental state a *mental* state is its function. What is the function of a mental state? According to most functionalists, the function of a mental state is to a play a certain *causal role*. What causal role? Standard functionalism claims that mental states in general have essentially three causal roles: (i) they are caused by sensory input, (ii) they cause behavioural output, and (iii) they are causes of and caused by other mental states. According to this view, mental state types are distinguished from one another (beliefs from desires from fears, etc.) by virtue of the particular causal profile that is characteristic of them (we will return to this in more detail in the final chapter). Notice that this characterization of a mental state is abstracted from the nature of the stuff that is needed to carry out the causal roles of any given mental state. Consider the mental state of belief, for example; in particular, my belief, say, that my hair is on fire. This belief is typically caused by various sensory stimulations – my looking in a mirror, feeling hot about the ears, smelling an odour or hearing people say 'Your hair is on fire!' – and typically causes me to have the desire to put the fire out; this desire, in turn, normally causes certain behaviour on my part, involving frantic flailing and rolling about. We just considered an attitude state; let us consider an experiential state, such as pain. Pain is normally caused by bodily damage and causes the belief that one is pain, the desire to rid oneself of the pain and behaviour believed to relieve the pain. These states of belief, desire and pain could, the functionalist thinks, be realized or implemented or embodied in any number of different ways: by neural synapses or silicon chips, just as a clock can be made out of rock (in the case of an sundial) or metal. Functionalists are usually materialists however, in the sense that they think mental states are in fact always embodied in some king of material medium.

Functionalism comes in many forms. It has many critics and the various issues and debates that surround it fill a vast amount of often complex and technical literature. It is beyond the scope of this book to do justice to these debates, but let us note two things about standard functionalism. First, on the positive side, notice that causal role (iii) enables functionalism to capture something that behaviourism left out: the fact that mental events cause other mental events. (Armstrong's identity theory is also able to account for this kind of mental causation.) Recall that, though Ryle was able to give a behavioural interpretation of the idea that there are mental causes, in one sense, by saying that publicly observable environmental conditions trigger behavioural dispositions (though even in this he was ultimately unsuccessful), he could give no behavioural interpretation of the idea that there are *mental processes*, such as one belief leading to another, a belief causing a desire, or simply thinking. Second, on the negative side, recall that Armstrong's claim that mental states are essentially causes of behaviour (causal role (ii)) is not beyond question. One can accept the claim that mental states are essentially causes and effects but reject the claim that they are essentially causes and effects of publicly observable events, such as perceptual stimuli and behaviour. It remains for you to decide which of causal roles (i)–(iii), if any, is essential to something's being one or another mental state and therefore how much of standard functionalism is acceptable.

Summary

Armstrong's identity theory attempts to synthesize the inner and the outer, the Cartesian and Rylean views of the mind, by holding, first, that mental states are by definition inner causes (of outward behaviour) and, second, that these inner states are in fact material states of the central nervous system. The first stage is conceptual and is carried out *a priori*; the second is empirical and is carried out *a posteriori*. The identity theory faces three central problems, however: (a) it is not clear whether it can account for the painfulness of pain, (b) it is not clear whether it must be behaviour that mental states necessarily cause, and (c) it must deal with the objection from multiple realizability. This last objection is one of the main forces driving functionalism: the view that mental states are functional states that play certain causal roles that are capable of multiple realization in a variety of different media.

Further reading

Armstrong's 'The nature of mind' is drawn from his collection of essays of the same title (1981). For a comprehensive presentation of his view see *A Materialist Theory of the Mind* (1968). A shorter presentation is his essay 'Consciousness and causality' in D.M. Armstrong and Norman Malcolm, *Consciousness and Causality* (1984). It is worth reading both Armstrong's and Malcolm's essays in this book, and their replies to each other, to get a good idea of two radically opposed views of the mind. Two other classic sources for the type identity theory are J.J.C. Smart's 'Sensations and brain processes', reprinted in Rosenthal's reader (1991), and U.T. Place's 'Is consciousness a brain process?', reprinted in Lycan's reader (1999). The most famous defence of a token identity thesis is Donald Davidson's difficult 'Mental events', reprinted in both Rosenthal and Lycan, and in a volume of Davidson's collected papers *Essays on Actions and Events* (1980). Both Lycan's and Rosenthal's readers contain classic functionalist writings. Kim's *Philosophy of Mind* (1996) and Guttenplan's *Mind's Landscape* (2000) offer excellent detailed and sustained critical accounts of functionalism. Braddon-Mitchell and Jackson's *Mind and Cognition* (1996) discusses various versions of functionalism and defends a distinctive version against objections. We have not had time to consider the general doctrine of materialism in any detail. Though it is certainly the orthodox view in contemporary analytical philosophy of mind, it should not be accepted uncritically. Scattered throughout the writings of the linguist and philosopher Noam Chomsky is an interesting critique of materialism and an argument to the effect that the mind–body problem has no coherent formulation. See, for example, chapter five of *Language and Problems of Knowledge* (1988, especially pages 138ff.) and the opening pages of 'Naturalism and dualism in the study of language and mind' and 'Language as a natural object', both in Chomsky's *New Horizons in the Study of Language and Mind* (2000). For critical reactions, see the first three essays in *Chomsky and his Critics*, edited by Louise Antony and Norbert Hornstein (2003). For an excellent critical examination of the idea of a purely physical conception of the world, see chapter three of Stroud (2000).

CHAPTER 5

The Big Idea – Thinking Matter

Armstrong and Fodor are interested in the project of seeing how mental phenomena, broadly construed, fit into the natural world as it is described by the natural sciences, with its mathematical and quantitative methods. They, and the majority of philosophers working in the analytical tradition, take the success of the empirical sciences in explaining an impressively wide range of phenomena very seriously. They think the same methods should be applied to mental phenomena. They are, then, what we might call 'methodological naturalists' who are interested in 'naturalizing the mind', that is, in showing how mental phenomena can be explained by natural science. This is something, of course, that Descartes denied was possible. You will recall that Armstrong tries to justify this stance, which he calls 'scientism', in the section of his essay entitled 'The authority of science'. You may wish to re-read this and consider whether you agree with it and how you would respond if you do not.

The issue of 'naturalism' is a large one and we do not have the space to consider it in detail here. Our aim is simply to explore in an introductory way what those philosophers who see themselves as naturalists are up to. One point, however, is worth making. This is that that it is fully compatible with methodological naturalism, which is simply a kind of 'pro-science' stance, that each science – physics, chemistry, biology, geology, psychology, etc. – is rigorously scientific in its methods but relatively autonomous, in the sense that it can carry out its business without worrying about its relationship to other sciences. Some naturalists adopt a stronger stance than mere methodological naturalism: they think the various sciences should 'fit together' and so they aim for some kind of integration or unification of science, or for something even stronger, such as the incorporation or reduction of one science into another. It is important to be aware of these different conceptions and to realize that the one does not necessarily follow from the other. It is one thing to believe that scientific methods are the best methods for studying some given phenomenon and quite another thing to believe that all scientific explanations and theories should fit together in some way or be reduced to one grand and unified total theory of everything.

Naturalism and cognitivism

The rise of methodological naturalism is a complex story. It is not just the undeniable success of empirical science in explaining previously recalcitrant phenomena, such as biological and chemical processes (the theory of evolution and the discovery of DNA, for example) that accounts for its appeal. Also at play here is probably the lingering influence of logical empiricism. The logical empiricists claimed that only statements for which it is clear how to go about verifying, confirming or testing are meaningful or significant. They combined deep admiration for science with contempt for metaphysical propositions, such as 'mental states are states of an immaterial substance that cause material happenings', because statements like this are not testable. Such statements are deeply problematic to many philosophers and scientists because they seem to put the mind beyond the reach of scientific study. With dualism, for example, there seems no way conclusively to confirm any propositions about the mind; we are at the mercy of a subject's introspective reports about his or her mental states – even granting that we can assume we are dealing with a subject at all and not simply an automaton! One need not accept the empiricists' claim that such metaphysical statements are literally meaningless to sympathize with their view that they are nevertheless very unsatisfactory because there seems no way to determine whether they are true.

The hard-nosed scientism of the logical empiricists was also present in a group of young psychologists around the turn of the last century, who described themselves as behaviourists, the most famous being J.B. Watson, who proclaimed in a 1913 article in the journal *Psychological Review*: 'Psychology as the behaviourist views it is a purely objective experimental branch of natural science' (in Lyons 1995, 24). The behaviourists wished to replace what they saw as the sterile and impotent introspectionist psychology current at the time, which was based on the self-examinational reports of subjects on their own mental states, with an objective methodology focused entirely on publicly observable events – namely, a subject's responses to environmental conditions. The goal of a truly scientific psychology, they thought, is, in the words of Watson, 'the prediction and control of behaviour' (ibid.). In such an endeavour no mention should be made of mental states, consciousness, mind, mental imagery and the like; the kinds of things the introspectionists were happy to embrace. All this is to be replaced with talk of publicly observable patterns of physical responses to physical stimuli. The programme was carried out in a revised and more sophisticated form by B.F. Skinner (1904–90).

This 'scientific behaviourism' (sometimes also called 'psychological behaviourism' or 'methodological behaviourism') is a form of naturalism. Alas, it suffers from much the same problems as Ryle's quasi-behaviourism and the logical positivists' logical behaviourism. It seems utterly incapable of accounting for what are clearly inner episodes or processes not accompanied by any behaviour, such as simply thinking. (Watson did hypothesize that thinking to oneself is talking to oneself 'sub-vocally' and thus a matter of the subtle movements of some of the muscles involved in speech. But this hypothesis was not borne out by the experimental findings.) Moreover, it fails on its own terms, for it seems incapable of explaining, let alone predicting or controlling, intelligent behaviour of any complexity – for example, radically novel behaviour and, the most recalcitrant of all to behaviourist treatment, language learning and use.

It is these shortcomings that were partly responsible for ushering in the next phase of naturalism. The failings of both scientific and logical behaviourism, together with the remarkable discoveries of neurophysiology in the first half of the twentieth century and the developments in the information sciences before and after the Second World War, led eventually to a new movement in psychology and philosophy of mind known as 'cognitivism' or sometimes 'mentalism'. Cognitivism is, very generally, the view that mind and mental phenomena cannot be understood without reference to internal mental states and processes. In opposition to the behaviourist, the cognitivist thinks that the only viable scientific psychology is one that embraces inner mental causal states and processes. We have already seen that Armstrong's central state materialism identifies mental states with neural processes. Other philosophers have tried to naturalize the mind by comparing it to a computer and this is the idea that we shall look at in the remainder of this chapter.

The causal–explanatory nature of mental phenomena

This cognitivist attitude is evident in Fodor's Preface to his book *Psychosemantics* (1987), in which he describes the behaviour of his cat and the theory that is the most likely explanation of this behaviour.

> I have, as it happens, a strikingly intelligent cat. Here are some of the behaviors in which his intelligence is manifest.
>
> In the morning, at his usual feeding time, Greycat prowls the area of the kitchen near his food bowl. When breakfast appears, he positions himself with respect to the bowl in a manner that facilitates ingestion.
>
> When the house is cold, Greycat often sleeps before the fireplace. But he does this only if there's a fire on the hearth, and he never gets close enough to singe his hair.
>
> When his foot encounters a sharp object, Greycat withdraws it. In similar spirit, he maintains an appreciable distance between himself and the nearest aggressive dog.
>
> He occasionally traps and disembowels small rodents.
>
> In saying that these behaviors manifest striking intelligence, I do not mean to imply that Greycat is at an intellectual advantage with respect to other cats. On the contrary, many cat owners have similar anecdotes to report. I allow for the hyperbole that their infatuation prompts, but by and large I believe them.
>
> No, my point is that Greycat is strikingly intelligent in comparison with, for example, rocks, trees, worms, and spiral nebulae. Rocks, trees, worms, and spiral nebulae are, each in its own way, quite complicated objects. Each has claimed the attention of some of our best scientific minds, and there are, no doubt, many things about them that we still don't understand. Yet none of their behaviors seems remotely as clever as Greycat's. In fact, they don't – excepting, maybe, grossly metaphorically – behave at all. Oh, mice have died, and worms have eaten them; but no rock, and no spiral nebula – and no worm, for that matter – has ever chased a mouse, let alone caught one. (Mousetraps catch mice, of course; but that manifests our intelligence, not theirs.)
>
> It seems to me to want explaining, this impressive difference between Greycat's behavioral capacities and those of, say, the spiral nebula in Andromeda. I have, as it happens, a strikingly intelligent theory.

> The theory is that Greycat – unlike rocks, worms, nebulae, and the rest – has, and acts out of, beliefs and desires. The reason, for example, that Greycat patrols his food bowl in the morning is that he wants food and believes – has come to believe on the basis of earlier feedings – that his food bowl is the place to find it. The reason that Greycat avoids aggressive dogs is that he is afraid of them. The reason that Greycat scratches at the door is that he wants out. And so forth. Whereas, by contrast, rocks and the like do not have beliefs and desires. Their 'behaviors' are different from Greycat's because they are, in this respect, differently caused.
>
> I have no serious doubt that this theory (what I call 'commonsense belief/desire) is pretty close to being true.
>
> (Fodor 1987, ix–x)

ACTIVITY

What is Fodor's 'strikingly intelligent theory', which he thinks explains Greycat's 'strikingly intelligent' behaviour?

DISCUSSION

The theory that Fodor thinks explains Greycat's behaviour is the theory that Greycat has beliefs and desires and other mental states and that these cause Greycat's behaviour. Greycat's behaviour of sitting near the fire is explained by ascribing to him the *desire* to be warm and the *belief* that sitting near the fire will make him warm. The reason why this belief and desire explain Greycat's behaviour is that they caused his behaviour. This 'commonsense belief/desire psychological' explanation is, for Fodor, just like any other causal explanation for the occurrence of an event. If we want to know why a certain event occurred – the collapse of some bridge, say – we look for the causes of the event, the things that brought it about – an earthquake, for example. Similarly, in order to explain the event of Greycat's coming to sit by the fire we need to know what its causes are; according to Fodor these causes include, inter alia, the aforementioned belief and desire. Greycat's behaviour cannot be understood in purely behaviouristic terms.

Fodor refers to the 'commonsense belief/desire psychology' or, as it is sometimes called, 'folk psychology', that explains Greycat's behaviour as a 'theory'. The fact that mental states, events and processes seem to play a causal–explanatory role in behaviour and that reference to mental states is part of a theory that we all use to explain and predict the actions and thoughts of our fellow creatures has played a central role in the philosophy of mind since the 1950s. This idea may strike you as slightly odd. How could the idea that people have mental states – beliefs, desires, emotions, fears, pains, jealousy and so on

– be a *theory*? Who invented or discovered the theory? When were the experiments performed? What are the laws of the theory? Have its founders been nominated for a Nobel Prize? There is no doubt that commonsense psychology is not a theory in the same sense in which the theory of evolution by natural selection, the theory of plate tectonics and the theory of quantum mechanics are theories. These theories have been consciously and explicitly thought up and formulated by individual scientists; they have been tested and confirmed by experiments; and they consist of a precise system of laws and concepts, many of which are rigorously mathematical. Commonsense psychology has none of these features. Nevertheless, in the eyes of many philosophers, including Fodor's, commonsense psychology is like a theory in the loose sense of being a conceptual and explanatory framework that we employ in our attempts to explain and predict, and generally make intelligible, the behaviour of our fellow creatures. The idea, the basis of which was first explicitly stated by the American philosopher Wilfrid Sellars (1912–89), is that beliefs, desires, fears, intentions and emotions are 'theoretical entities', which are unobservable, and which we 'postulate' as occurring inside people as the causes of their behaviour, in the same way that electrons and genes are unobservable theoretical entities postulated by physicists and biologists, respectively, to explain the behaviour of matter and living organisms. Moreover, the theoretical postulates of commonsense psychology – beliefs, desires and other mental states – are embedded in a network of rough law-like generalizations. We know, for example, that creatures that desire food and believe food to be located in a certain place generally move, or at least try to move, their bodies, to that place. People who have headaches generally desire to get rid of them; and if they also believe certain substances will rid them of their headaches they take those substances. This 'theory' is not, of course, explicitly held and consciously developed by us in the way that theoretical research programs are in universities throughout the world. Some philosophers and psychologists hold that our knowledge of the theory is supposed to be largely tacit or implicit: it is deeply embedded in our ways of thinking and we are not necessarily able to annunciate or even recognize most of the underlying principles of the theory.

This 'theory' view – or, as it is sometimes called, the 'theory theory' – of our predictive and explanatory capacities as commonsense psychologists is rejected by a substantial number of philosophers. Some philosophers deny that we predict, explain and generally make intelligible the thoughts and behaviour of our fellow creatures by deploying a theory. They think, instead,

empathy

that we are able to make sense of people's thoughts and behaviour because we have a sympathetic or empathetic ability to project ourselves imaginatively into other people's shoes and 'simulate' their states of mind. This is the 'simulation theory' of commonsense psychology. There are yet other views about the nature of commonsense psychology. John Searle, for example, who is well known for his trenchant critique of some of the aspirations of cognitive science, considers the idea that we postulate beliefs and desires completely ridiculous; on the contrary, he says, 'we do not *postulate* beliefs and desires to account for anything. We simply experience conscious beliefs and desires... They are no more postulated than conscious pains' (Searle 1992, 59). Wherever the truth of the matter lies, for our purposes it is important to note that the theory view of commonsense psychology holds that commonsense psychology is an *empirical* theory. This means that it is possible that the theory is false. That is to say, to hold that commonsense psychology is an empirical theory about the causes of human and animal behaviour is to commit oneself to the possibility that the causes of human behaviour – talking and walking, building bridges, running companies, and composing symphonies and sonnets – are not in fact beliefs and desires or any mental states at all. It could turn out, on this view, that a completed or advanced neurophysiology discovers that of all the internal states of humans and animals none of them corresponds to anything like what commonsense psychology takes to be mental states. If this happened then it would turn out that there were no mental states; such things simply do not exist. No one, strictly speaking, has ever believed, feared or remembered anything! 'Belief', 'desire', 'fear', 'memory', and the rest of the mental states would be mythical entities like witches, demons, the four humours, phlogiston and caloric – there simply are no such things. They are the mistaken posits of a false theory of the causation of human behaviour.

This possibility is taken seriously by some philosophers of mind known as eliminative materialists. These philosophers think that commonsense psychology (or 'folk psychology') is, or is very likely, a false empirical theory of a piece with the moribund theories in the dustbin of the history of science, such as the phlogiston theory of combustion or the caloric theory of heat or the Ptolemaic theory of planetary motion. These eliminative materialists endorse the elimination of commonsense psychology and its mental categories and advocate its eventual replacement by neuroscience or some other science. If this seems incredible to you then you are in good company, for Fodor too thinks that it is incredible. As he says, if commonsense psychology 'were to collapse, that would be, beyond comparison, the greatest intellectual catastrophe in the history of our species' (1987, xii). Nevertheless, it is important to emphasize that, though Fodor differs from the eliminative materialists in holding that commonsense psychology is a true theory, he is still committed to the possibility that it may be entirely false. He thus differs sharply from Searle who thinks that, while it is possible that commonsense psychology might have turned out to be false, we know in fact that it is not, because we already know we have beliefs, desires and pains – each one of us is aware of having them. As we shall see, Fodor argues that there are good reasons to be optimistic about commonsense psychology's claim to truth. His main project, which he has defended for two decades or so, is to 'vindicate' commonsense psychology by showing that the prospects for an explicit scientific theory of thought and behaviour, a *real* theory, that employs mentalistic concepts, such as belief, desire, fear and intention, are in fact very good. He wants a scientific theory that explains how belief and desires, and the rest of the mental states of commonsense psychology, could cause behaviour. Fodor wants to know what kind of *mechanism* it is exactly that connects mental states with each other and to behaviour. If mental states are like the states of a computer, Fodor argues, then commonsense psychology will be vindicated because computational states are precisely the sorts of things that can have the causal–explanatory properties that commonsense psychology takes mental states to have.

Before we turn to the theory, we need to see just what Fodor takes beliefs, desires, etc. to be – according to commonsense psychology. When we see what mental states are supposed to be like, according to this view, we will be in a better position to see why Fodor holds his theory, why he thinks that the mind is, essentially, a kind of computer.

Causation and content in commonsense psychology

To the question 'How do we tell whether a psychology *is* a belief/desire psychology?', Fodor answers that it must be one that postulates states that have (i) representational content and (ii) causal powers. Let us take each of these ideas in turn.

Representational content as an essential feature of commonsense psychology

In Chapter 1, we noted that attitudes, such as belief, are *about* or *directed at* various things, such as objects and states of affairs. They have intentionality. Thus Churchill can be admired by me but loathed by you and loved by his wife and children. The state of affairs of Churchill being Prime Minister can be believed, feared or wished for. Fodor thinks that whenever we have an attitude to something we represent it in a certain way. Shifting from British politics to the somewhat more exciting world of ancient Greek tragedy, consider the fact that Oedipus married the queen of Thebes, Jocasta, not realizing she was his mother. After the ceremony, Oedipus thinks of Jocasta as *his wife* and as *the queen of Thebes* but most certainly not as *his mother* (even though she is, tragically, his mother). It is part of Oedipus' story about Jocasta, part of the way he takes the world to be, that she is his wife and not his mother. In other words, he represents her as his wife and not as his mother. At the moment of his tragic realization, his *anagnorisis,* he comes to represent her as his wife *and* his mother – and his behaviour changes radically. Thus the power of mental representation: the difference between an Oedipus who is about to put out his own eyes and an Oedipus who is not, is a representation, namely, *my wife is my mother (!)*. Fodor's point is that commonsense psychology explains the behaviour of creatures like Oedipus and Greycat by attributing representational states to them; for how they represent things determines how they will behave toward them. When philosophers speak of the phenomenon of intentionality they are referring to this feature of thoughts by which they reach out to or aim at or represent things beyond themselves. It is in this sense that commonsense psychology ascribes 'intentional' or 'representational' states to creatures with a view to explaining, predicting and generally making intelligible their behaviour.

Philosophers sometimes speak of the representational feature of our attitudes as their *content* and of that content or representation having a *semantic evaluation*. That is, since attitudes represent things beyond themselves, they can be evaluated with respect to whether these things beyond themselves are as they are represented to be. In other words, we can always ask whether the content of an attitude fits with reality. Thus my belief that Descartes was a scientific genius is about a certain man having a certain property – namely, Descartes's being a scientific genius – and this is the *content* of my belief. This content of my belief – which in this case is specified by a declarative statement or proposition, namely, the proposition *that Descartes is a scientific genius* – can be evaluated with respect to whether it matches reality. If the content of my belief does match reality – namely, if Descartes was indeed a scientific genius – then that content can be evaluated as true, and if it does not match, as false. The evaluation is a *semantic* one because it concerns the relation between the belief and the world just as the semantics of a language concerns the relation between the signs of the language and their meanings, that is, what they signify. As we shall see later, Fodor not only thinks that attitudes have semantics but also, controversially, that they have syntax (grammar). So it is important to keep in mind the distinction between the semantic and the syntactic properties of signs; the former is a sign–world relation, the latter a sign–sign relation.

Evaluating an attitude, or the content of an attitude, as true or false is not the only kind of semantic evaluation. Desires too can be evaluated semantically; as can hopes, wishes, expectations and intentions. Desires can be satisfied or unsatisfied, wishes and hopes fulfilled or unfulfilled, expectations met or unmet and intentions carried out or not carried out. In order to evaluate a desire semantically, we would need to find out whether it was satisfied and this would involve investigating the world to see whether it was brought to conform to the desire. For example, suppose my sister wants to have a baby. In order semantically to evaluate this mental state, this desire, we need to find out whether she succeeds in this endeavour. (We could also evaluate her desire on the basis of whether it is a good or a bad desire to have, but that would not be a *semantic* evaluation).

An explanatory psychological scheme counts as being a commonsensical one only if it involves the postulation of states part of whose nature is to be true or false, satisfied or unsatisfied, and so on – in short, states with content that represent the world as being a certain way and thus are semantically evaluable. This is what sets commonsense psychology off from other explanatory schemes, such as physics, which explains the behaviour of small particles and spiral nebulae without attributing to them states which are true or false, satisfied or unsatisfied. Fodor is not saying that *every* state postulated by a psychology purporting to be commonsensical must have representational content; only that among the states it does postulate at least some of them must. Thus he allows for purely experiential mental states without any attitudinal or intentional component – if there are such things. Some philosophers think that some moods, for example, anxiety or depression, do not have any intentionality because they are not directed at anything in particular. When I have a case of 'the blues', when I'm 'feeling down', I may not be depressed about anything in particular, and so it may not make sense to ask whether my state of mind is a correct or incorrect representation of reality. These kinds of mental states, if such there be, do not appear to be susceptible to a semantic evaluation, for they are not about anything in particular. Fodor can allow for this, so long as these kinds of states are said by the psychology in question to exist alongside states that are susceptible of semantic evaluation. Moreover, he can also allow for the possibility that those states that have representational content (i.e. that are semantically evaluable) may also have other features as well, such as experiential ones, as some philosophers argue that emotions and perceptions have (recall the discussion of the variety and possible heterogeneity of mental phenomena in Chapter 1).

ACTIVITY

Can you think of any other things that represent, that have content?

DISCUSSION

The most obvious thing that comes to mind is linguistic symbols. Declarative sentences, for example, whether written, spoken, or given in sign language, have content. They say something about the world and can be evaluated with respect to whether what they say is true, just like beliefs. Notice that linguistic symbols' representational powers are owed entirely to the use we put them, usually in a conventional system of representation. The sentence 'Aquinas never met Elvis' means what it does because we use it to mean that. The French and the Germans use different symbols to say the very same thing. Similarly, symbols such as maps, diagrams, signs, signals, gestures, codes and musical notation are conventional symbols in that they represent what they do because we so use them.

Another kind of representation is pictorial representation: pictures, drawings, paintings, sculpture, etchings, engravings, photographs and the visual arts generally. Just how much of the representational power of pictures is owed to convention and how much to resemblance is a controversial issue in aesthetics.

As we shall see, Fodor thinks that the content of our attitudes derives from the content of a special non-conventional representational system, a 'language of thought'.

A puzzling feature of representations is that, not only can they be false by misrepresenting the world, but they can represent what does not exist.

Paintings, for example, often represent things that do not exist, such as dragons and other mythical beasts. Importantly, for philosophers of mind, mental states can represent what does not exist. I can believe Vulcan is a planet and that Ossian was a poet; I can wish that phlogiston was responsible for combustion, wonder whether Piltdown Man hunted deer. A child can think about Santa Claus. All this even though none of these things exists. Philosophers find this feature of representation deeply perplexing. After all, representation seems to be a relation; but relations can only obtain between things that exist. If 'x danced with y' is true then x and y must exist. But in order for 'x represents y' to be true, y does not have to exist. If it were really true that, for example, Arch Stanton danced with Santa Claus then Santa Claus must exist. How else could Arch dance with him? Since Santa Claus does not exist it cannot be (literally) true that Arch danced with him. But it seems that we can have thoughts about things that do not exist, and thus represent those things, even if we cannot dance with them. While it is false that Arch Stanton danced with Santa Claus, it may well be true that Little Archie is thinking about, and hence representing, Santa Claus.

Many philosophers call the mental states we have been calling attitudes or states with intentionality or states that represent, such as beliefs and desires, *propositional attitudes*. This is because many mental states can be described by statements that appear to relate subjects to whole propositions. For example, we might say what Stanton believed by saying Stanton believed *that the gun was not loaded*. What follows the 'that' expresses a proposition, in this case, the proposition *the gun was not loaded*. Stanton can have any number of different attitudes to this proposition; he might *hope* that the gun is not loaded, *fear* that the gun is not loaded and so on. In this sense, propositions are said to give or specify the *content* of someone's belief; propositions tell us *what it is* that they believe. The representational content of an attitude is often given by a proposition.

ACTIVITY

Consider the various kinds of attitudes, some of which were mentioned in Chapter 1. Can the content of an attitude always be described by a proposition? (Hint: consider the content of emotional attitudes.)

DISCUSSION

Though talk of 'propositional attitudes' is ubiquitous and *de rigueur* in the philosophy of mind and language, caution should be exercised. For it is far from clear that the content of all intentional or attitudinal states can be given by mentioning a proposition (expressed by a declarative sentence) to which the subject in question has the attitude in question. Many emotions, for example, do not appear to have propositional content. Love, hate, admiration, worship, and fondness do not seem easily described with the use of propositions. Stanton *loves Rosie* and *admires Burton*. What follow the attitude verbs 'loves' and 'admires' here are not declarative sentences expressing propositions but proper names of objects, namely, people. The 'content' of these emotional attitudes does not seem to be propositional, at least not if we take these linguistic expression at face value. Nevertheless, philosophers often talk as if all the attitudes are propositional in nature and it is important to be aware of this over-simplification.

We have before us a bewildering variety of terms which are employed to characterize, in one way or another, attitudes: 'intentional states', 'propositional attitudes', 'states with content', 'states with representational content', 'representational states', 'semantically evaluable states' and even 'meanings'. Though all these are subtly different we can, for our purposes, treat them as all roughly the same: they are simply different ways of referring to those mental states, which we have been calling attitudes, that point beyond themselves to something else that has content.

Mental causation as an essential feature of commonsense psychology

Commonsense psychology, according to Fodor, is committed to the view that mental states – especially attitudes – are causes and effects: my perception of a pig in my kitchen can cause me to come to believe that there is a pig in my kitchen and this belief may in turn cause further mental states, such as my wondering why there is a pig in my kitchen. My wondering may cause me to remember that I left the kitchen door open after burning some toast. All these thoughts may eventually terminate in some behaviour of mine, such as trying to scare the pig away. Generally speaking, mental states cause other mental states, they cause behaviour and they are caused by perceptual input. So, we have two essential features of attitudes: they have representational content, which is semantically evaluable, and they have causal powers. But we have yet to reach the most important fact about the content and causation of mental states.

Causation by content in commonsense psychology: how is rationality mechanically possible?

It is an extremely important fact for Fodor – a fundamental assumption underlying his entire project – that a given mental state has both content and is a cause and effect. As he puts it, with his own emphasis, commonsense psychology 'attributes contents and causal powers *to the very same mental things that it takes to be semantically evaluable*' (1987, 12). But there is an even deeper point Fodor is at pains to emphasize, which is that an attitude with a certain content often causes another attitude with a different content in such a way that the first content is *rationally related* to the second. The first content, for example, might logically entail the second or it might stand in some kind of evidential relation of support to it. Another way of putting this is to say that attitudes such as beliefs and desires are not only causes of further mental states and behaviour but also *reasons* for having those further mental states and engaging in that behaviour. One of Fodor's favourite examples of causation by content is Sherlock Holmes's famous feats of detection. If Holmes thinks the victim was killed by a snake and that the only snakes in the vicinity are those owned by the doctor, then he has a reason to draw the conclusion, to believe, that one of the doctor's snakes killed the victim. The first two beliefs are both *reasons* for the third *and* the *cause* of Holmes's coming to the third.

It is not just that Holmes's belief that the victim was killed by a snake and the only snakes in the vicinity are those owned by the doctor *causes* Holmes's belief that one of the doctor's snakes killed the victim, but that the *content* of the first belief (the victim was killed by a snake and the only snakes in the vicinity are those owned by the doctor) is *rationally related* to the *content* of the second belief (one of the doctor's snakes killed the victim). There is a parallelism or harmony between, on the one hand, the causal powers of mental states and, on the other hand, the rational relations between the contents of these causally related mental states. Fodor likes to stress that without this harmony there would be little point in thinking. For if my mental processes were not largely rational then I could never reason successfully about anything, never deduce anything and never act rationally in the light of my knowledge. There is not much point in thinking, for example, the true thoughts 'All humans are mortals' and 'Fodor is human' if having these thoughts causes me to think a thought rationally unrelated to them, such as 'Fodor is immortal' or even worse 'Grass is purple', instead of one that is rationally related to them (in this case *logically entailed* by them), such as 'Fodor is mortal'. For, if the thought that gets caused is rationally related to the thought that did the causing, then if the first thought is true the second thought will be true too. Good thinking is precisely that which takes us from truths to other truths by making sure that the connections between the thoughts in the thinking are rational ones. Of course, not all mental processes are rational, for obviously non-rational trains of thought occur, such as free association. Nevertheless, many, perhaps most, of our thought processes are rational. But how could they be? As Fodor puts it:

> I'm suggesting – or rather I'm endorsing what I take to be Conan Doyle's very acute suggestion – that, whatever else a mind may be, it is some sort of rationality machine. So, now, given the methodological commitment to materialism, the question arises, how a machine could be rational? At a minimum, how could a purely physical system be so organized that if it starts in a state of believing something true, its causal processes will lead it to other true beliefs?
>
> (Fodor 1992, 6)

The answer: the computational theory of mind

Fodor is a standard functionalist in the sense that he thinks that what makes a state of a creature a mental state is its function, which he takes to be its causal role (recall that there are three general causal roles associated with mental states according to standard functionalism – see page 78 above). That is, he thinks that what makes a mental state a state of belief as opposed, say, to a state of desire is the way the state in question interacts with other states and perception and behaviour. Belief states will have different causal roles from desire states and that is what makes them beliefs instead of desires. It is very important, however, to separate this functionalist account of what makes a certain state a mental state of a certain kind (a belief rather than a desire) from the very different question of what makes a particular state, such as a particular belief or a particular desire, have the mental content that it does. In other words, we can ask what makes it the case that a certain belief of mine is the belief *that reptiles are cold blooded* rather than the belief *that mammals are warn blooded*. This is a question about the *content* of a particular mental state, a belief in this case, and the question is what determines its content. It is possible to be a functionalist about mental content as well as being a functionalist about mental state types. A functionalist about mental content thinks, roughly speaking, that the content of a mental state is determined by its relations to the contents of other mental states, and different accounts are given of what these relations are (they might be, for example, inferential relations). This theory of mental content is sometime called 'functional role semantics' or 'conceptual role semantics' (in cognitive science, one version of it goes under the name of 'procedural semantics') because it claims that the semantics, that is, the content, the representational properties, of mental states are determined by their functional role. Fodor, however, while being a functionalist about mental state types (about what makes a state a belief rather than a desire) rejects functionalism about mental content, holding that the content of a mental state is determined ultimately by a special kind of relation it bears to what it represents in the world (rather than its relations to the contents of other mental states). One should always be careful to distinguish between functionalism about mental state types and functionalism about mental content.

What is distinctive about Fodor's functionalist view is the theory he has of how, in humans and other animals, mental states are implemented or incarnated; that is, how they are able to perform their function, how they are able to be causes and effects of perceptual input, other mental states and behavioural output. Fodor's theory about how this is possible is that the mind is a kind of computer and that mental states are computational states. His answer to the above questions involves *the computational theory of mind* (CTM). There are two key parts to CTM: representation and computation. Let us take the representational part of the theory first.

Representation

The idea behind the representational part of the theory is that there is a set of mental symbols ('mental representations') whose causal interaction with one another constitutes mental processes. This set of mental symbols is known as the 'language of thought' or 'mentalese'. Thinking, according to CTM, is done in a language; not a natural language, like English, but a language of thought. Intentional states are relations to the 'mental sentences' of this language of thought and these mental sentences have propositions as their meanings, just as the ordinary written or spoken sentences of English have propositions as their meanings (the English sentence 'Mammals are warm blooded' has as its meaning the proposition that mammals are warm blooded, the same proposition that the appropriate French and Italian sentences also have as their meanings). These propositions, in turn, may or may not be about ordinary external objects, depending on whether any such things answer to the subject matter of the proposition. To believe *P* is to have a mental representation that means *P* activated in your head in a certain way. Assuming the truth of physicalism, CTM supposes that, in humans and animals, it is various neural events in the brain that constitute activating a mental representation, though other physical materials, such as silicon chips, might do just as well. So there are 'neural words' and 'neural sentences' in the head that get produced during thinking; indeed, thinking just is a causal chain of such neural events. Believing *P* as opposed to desiring *P* consists of the neural sentence that means *P* being activated in your head in certain way. Believing *P* as opposed to believing *Q* consists in having the neural sentence that means *P* rather than the one that means *Q* activated in your head in a certain way. The belief that *P* and the belief that (if *P* then *Q*) giving rise to the belief that *Q* consists in the mentalese sentence that means *P* and the mentalese sentence that means (if *P* then *Q*) causing the mentalese sentence that means *Q* to be activated.

ACTIVITY

Fodor is a functionalist who thinks the same kind of mental state could in principle be 'realized' in a variety of different media – neurons, silicon chips, and even immaterial substances. However, he does not think that mental states are in fact ever incarnated in immaterial substances but always in various different kinds of material ones. So Fodor is a materialist who thinks that all mental states are ultimately physical. Does this make him a type identity or merely a token identity theorist?

DISCUSSION

It makes him merely a token identity theorist because he maintains that each token mental state is in fact identical with a token physical state, while denying that each token mental state of a certain type is identical with a token of the same type of physical state.

But, how is it that the neural symbols of mentalese cause each other in ways that preserve the rational relations between their meanings or representational contents? In other words, how, according to CTM, does it happen that a mental state that causes another mental state or a bit of behaviour is also a reason for that mental state or that behaviour? We want our theory to explain why it is that people are very often caused to believe *Q* by believing *P* when *P* *entails* *Q*. If CTM can explain how mental causation and mental content are kept in sync it will have gone a substantial way toward both vindicating commonsense psychology and showing how a scientific cognitive psychology is possible. The big idea about how rationality is 'mechanically possible' is owed to the great British mathematician Alan Turing (1912–54), whose work on computers during the Second World War helped to crack the German's Enigma Code. According to Fodor, Turing's idea is 'the most important idea about how the mind works that anybody has ever had' (Fodor 1992, 6).

Computation

'The trick', Fodor tells us, 'is to combine the postulation of mental representations with the "computer metaphor". Computers show us how to connect semantical with causal properties for *symbols*. So, if having a propositional attitude involves tokening [i.e. activating] a symbol, then we can get some leverage on connecting semantical properties with causal ones for *thoughts*' (1987, 18).

The key to explaining how mental causation and mental content are kept in sync is the notion of a computational process, the second part of CTM, and it brings out the full power of the 'language of thought' hypothesis. The big idea is that mental processes are computational processes, which means that they involve the automatic manipulation of symbols according to a fixed set of rules. Thinking and other mental processes, according to this view, are a matter of the manipulation of symbols, namely, the mental representations that are the sentences of mentalese. The key point to notice about the idea of a computational operation on a symbol is that the operation is performed on the basis of the symbol's non-semantic (i.e., non-representational) properties; for example, it might be performed on the basis of the physical properties of the symbol, such as its shape or weight or electrical conductivity. These non-semantic properties are among the symbol's *syntactic* properties. Computing machines are precisely machines built to detect the syntactic properties of symbols and to move the symbols around on the basis of their syntactic properties according to rules. Turing's great discovery was that we can build machines in such a way that the operations performed on the syntactic structures of the symbols preserve the rational relations between the representational contents of the symbols.

Let us look at this idea in more detail. Assume, for illustrative purposes only, that the symbols on which computational processes operate are shaped like letters. (In real digital computers the computations are performed on symbols written in binary machine code, which consists of strings of 0s and 1s, which are in turn implemented by electronic switches.) The idea is that since the symbol '*P*&*Q*' has a syntactic structure, which we can think of as its shape, it is possible to arrange things so that it causes the symbols '*P*' and '*Q*' to be produced, but not to cause the symbols 'not-*P*' and 'not-*Q*' to be produced, and to do so solely in virtue of shapes of all these symbols. All we need is a fixed set of rules that tells the computer how to manipulate such shapes. The very shapes of the symbols, so to speak, determines which other symbols they can interact with, just as the shape of a key determines which locks it will open, to use Fodor's analogy. Hence, so long as we give the computer the right set of rules, the causal relations between the syntactic structures (the shapes) of the mental symbols '*P*&*Q*', '*P*', '*Q*', 'not-*P*,' 'not-*Q*', will coincide with the rational relations between the propositions they express. That is to say, for example, that since '*P*&*Q*' entails both '*P*' and '*Q*', but not 'not-*P*' or 'not-*Q*', there could be an automatic mechanical process designed to follow rules so that when the physical symbol '*P*&*Q*' was encountered the processes only caused symbols with the physical shapes '*P*' and '*Q*' to occur but not symbols with the physical shapes 'not-*P*' and 'not-*Q*'. A computational process is precisely one that transforms symbols solely on the basis of their syntax. If the 'language of thought' hypothesis is correct, in that for some types of mental content there corresponds a symbolic representation with a syntactic structure, then my having different thoughts with this content at various times will always correspond to syntactic differences that make a causal difference in the production of further thought and behaviour. It is essential to CTM that two attitudes can differ in content only if they are implemented by distinct syntactically structured mental representations; for only then can the rational relations between their contents be preserved by a computational process that is sensitive only to the syntactic properties of the mental representations.

CTM is a kind of 'computational functionalism': mental states are defined by their causal roles and these causal roles are implemented by computational processes (which marry semantics and causation via syntax). These computational processes are then physically embodied in the neural 'wetware' of the human and animal brain or the silicon 'hardware' of the computer. CTM is an empirical hypothesis about how the matter of which humans and other animals are composed (especially our brains) actually thinks. We do not yet know whether it is true but Fodor is betting that it is at least to a certain extent on the right lines.

The scope and limits of CTM and a look beyond

There are many things to be said about CTM; it is controversial and is open to many different kinds of powerful criticism. It also has a serious competitor in the form of the rival approach known as 'connectionism' or 'parallel distributed processing', which does not view the brain as a symbol manipulator but rather as a complex system of multi-layered networks that purport to be more biologically accurate models of the brain's 'neural networks'. Some of this debate can be followed up in the suggestions for further reading and we will not go into it here. Instead I must draw the book to a close with a consideration of some of the issues that continue to occupy philosophers of mind. I will do this by discussing very briefly the scope and limits of CTM: just how many aspects of the mind can it account for?

Reasoning

I have been referring to the relations between the representational content of attitude states as 'rational' and discussing how these rational relations can be kept in sync with causal relations. But what is a 'rational' relation? When does a mental process count as reasoning? Philosophers distinguish between theoretical rationality and practical rationality. Theoretical rationality has as its goal true belief; we use theoretical rationality to decide what to *believe*. Practical rationality has as its goal appropriate action; we use it to decide what to *do*. Let us focus on theoretical rationality for a moment.

We can distinguish among three types of theoretical reasoning: deductive, inductive and abductive. A deductive inference is one in which we move from one or more premises to a conclusion logically entailed by it or them (for example, from the premises that all ravens are black and Arch is a raven to the conclusion that Arch is black). An inductive inference is one in which we move from a premise about some observed cases to a conclusion about some unobserved cases, as when we generalize from a representative sample to the population as a whole (for example, we infer that all ravens are black from the fact that all the many observed ravens have been black). An abductive inference is one in which we move, or leap, from some body of data to the best explanation for the data (this kind of reasoning is often called 'inference to the best explanation'). Abduction is the most pervasive kind of commonsense and scientific reasoning. Physicists, for example, infer the existence of 'dark matter' as the best explanation for certain cosmological facts about the motions of stars and galaxies. Similarly, a jury may infer that the defendant is the thief as the best explanation for why the diamonds were found in his safe with his fingerprints on them. In neither induction nor abduction is the conclusion logically entailed by the premises or data; the truth of the premises does not absolutely guarantee the truth of the conclusion with induction and abduction, in the way that it does with deduction.

We know from the work of Turing and others that many logically deductive inferences can be implemented computationally. But what about the far more pervasive forms of theoretical reasoning involving induction and abduction? The fact is that the project of mechanizing induction and abduction has not been nearly as successful as the mechanization of deduction. As things stand now, there are no known computational processes by which inductive and abductive reasoning of any sophistication can be implemented. Nor is there any kind of computational device that can engage in the most banal of decision making, such as what to do when you want a beer and there is no beer in the 'fridge – let alone which stocks to buy or even who to consult about which stocks to buy.

Now, the examples Fodor gives of reasoning processes found in commonsense psychology are inevitably non-deductive. The passages from Conan Doyle that Fodor often quotes are examples of abduction. Despite Sherlock Holmes's reputation as a master of deduction, he is, strictly speaking, a master of abduction. On the one hand, it is a very good example because it represents the pervasive presence of abductive inference in commonsense psychology. On the other hand, however, as Fodor himself sometimes points out, what we know from modern logic is that certain entailment relations – that is, *logically deductive* relations – can be 'mimicked' by syntactic relations – not abductive ones. Strictly speaking, then, CTM does not explain how Sherlock Holmes's reasoning processes could be carried out mechanically. CTM provides an explanation only for that small core of commonsense reasoning that is deductive. It is very much an open question how much of our reasoning processes are and can be carried out computationally, though it cannot be denied that the basic idea of computation keeping content and causation together is very suggestive about how reasoning in general might be mechanically possible.

Emotions

Some disturbing but fascinating cases of people with brain damage and mental illness were briefly discussed in the first chapter. These cases, as well some recent research in neuroscience, seem to suggest that the emotions may play a significant part in the higher cognitive functions of human beings and other animals. It seems that disruption to those areas of the brain and nervous system that are involved in emotions can greatly impair rationality. Yet the picture suggested by CTM is that emotions play very little role, if any, in thinking. Indeed, one could be forgiven for concluding that emotions, according to CTM, are entirely irrelevant to cognition. Is it that emotions are in fact computational processes but that CTM has simply left them out of its picture of thinking? Or is it rather that emotions cannot be explained computationally and that CTM is in need of supplementation if it is to provide an account of how humans and animals are able to think and reason. If the latter, then what kind of supplementation might this be? Well, another thing we noted about emotions in the first chapter was that some of them seem to involve an experiential element, often a visceral one, and are thus connected very intimately to the kinds of bodies we have, to the fact that we are made of flesh and blood rather than silicon chips. Could it be, then, that if emotions turn out to resist capture by computation, the kind of supplementation that CTM needs is a biological one? Could our minds be more tied to our biological makeup than computational functionalism suggests?

How do mental representations get their meaning?

There are two parts to CTM: a claim about the nature of mental states (they are relations to symbolic representations) and a claim about the nature of mental processes (they are computational). We have been focusing on the second part. But what about the first part? One pressing question that arises concerns how these mental representations get their meanings. According to CTM, to believe that Turing cracked the Enigma code, is to have a mental symbol in you (in the case of humans, in our heads, probably our brains) that means, or has the content, *that Turing cracked the Enigma code*. But how does it get this meaning or content? How is it that a neural configuration in my brain manages to be about Turing and the Enigma code? This is one form that the problem of intentionality can take: how can thoughts be directed at things, especially when those things need not exist? I mentioned very briefly above (p.9) that 'functional role semantics' has a story to tell about this and that Fodor has his own very different story. John Searle promotes a form of 'biological naturalism' according to which intentionality is essentially a biological phenomenon, somehow produced by brains. The point, however, is that even if Fodor is right, against Searle, that thinking is computation, the question how this thinking gets tied to its subject matter, how it manages to be about anything in the world, remains wide open.

Imagination and creativity

We are not only rational, emotional and conscious creatures, but also creative and imaginative ones. Indeed, it would be no exaggeration to say that that the greatest achievements of humankind, in both the arts and sciences (and philosophy!), are the product of creativity and imagination. Can creativity be understood computationally? Some philosophers think it can. These philosophers do not necessarily think that a computer, even a computer far more complex than the ones now in existence, could actually be creative. They do not necessarily think that creative processes of thought are computational processes. But they do think that computational processes, and computer simulations, may help us understand the nature of creativity. This approach obviously depends on how one thinks of creativity and imagination and these are topics that contemporary philosophers of mind are only beginning to investigate in any detail.

Consciousness

Emotions are not the only aspect of mind that involves an experiential element. As we saw in Chapter 1, sensations and perceptions involve the having of conscious experiences; there is 'something that it is like' to have sensations and experiences. Moreover, there is even something it is like to think: we all know what it is like to lie in bed at night thinking about how to solve some problem we must face in the morning. CTM seems to leave out entirely the experiential side of mental life. Can conscious experience be accounted for computationally? The answer to this question depends on whether conscious experience can be understood as representational, for computations are preformed on syntactically structured symbolic representations. If the smell of coffee and the pain of a headache are representational states then perhaps they can be understood computationally. A related question is whether consciousness can be understood functionally or whether it is essentially a biological phenomenon, as some philosophers, such as Searle, think. A larger question receiving much attention by philosophers is whether consciousness is even a physical phenomenon at all. Whether consciousness can be accounted for computationally, functionally, biologically or physically is another area of intense philosophical investigation.

Summary and an Aristotelian–Thomist reprise

Let us step back and consider the course we have followed. We have seen how Descartes's ancient and medieval predecessors considered mind to be essentially the rational activities of the intellect and will and that they tended to think no material substance could have these properties. The rational soul was independent of the body. Sensations and perceptions, however, were purely bodily processes and so not, strictly speaking, mental, if what we mean by 'mental' is what is associated with the rational soul. They do, however, transmit information to the rational soul for processing and manipulation. Descartes redrew these boundaries, repackaging as mental all and only those states of which we are indubitably aware, which included not only rational states but sensational ones as well. For Descartes, anything of which we are indubitably aware – which is transparently before consciousness – must be a state or property of an immaterial substance which can exist independently from any body. For behaviourists, mental states are essentially properties of material bodies, namely, their behaviours and dispositions to behaviour (though we noted some difficulty with interpreting Ryle as a behaviourist). Whereas Descartes sees the link between mind and body as causal and contingent, the behaviourist views it as non-causal and necessary: mental states are not causes of behaviour, they are the behaviour. Central state materialism or the type identity theory, as defended by Armstrong, views mental states as essentially causes of behaviour and hypothesizes that the causes of behaviour are neural events and processes. The functionalist views mental states as functional states whose nature is given by the *role* they play in a creature's mental life. Among the roles that mental states play are the causation of behaviour and other mental states as well as being the effects of sensory stimuli and other mental states. Functionalists think that since the essence of a given mental state is its job description, as it were, what it does for the organization that has it, psychological theorizing can abstract from all the various kinds of systems that implement or 'realize' the mental states. They are willing to grant the possibility of disembodied minds, extraterrestrial minds and machine minds but think that the hardware that implements the software or program of the mind – spiritual substance, nervous tissue, silicon chips – is largely irrelevant to the nature of many important aspects of mentality. The essence of mentation can be studied independently of knowing about how the hardware of an organism's body works. How, exactly, abstractly characterized functional relations are concretely set up in the minds of actual individuals is a job for whichever science deals with the kind of hardware in question: neuroscience in the case of earthly organisms, electrical engineering in the case of certain machines, and perhaps some yet-to-be-begun biology in the case of extraterrestrials.

Standard functionalism is, then, profoundly unbiological. In this sense it is very Cartesian: it separates mind from life. Descartes of course thought of the mind as an immaterial substance, which God attaches to material bodies. Functionalists think of the mind as an abstract structure of interrelated states that are defined by their overall role in the structure and this structure can be incarnated, and probably always is, in material bodies. Nevertheless, on both views, mentality can be embodied in non-living things. In considering the scope and limits of Fodor's CTM, however, I mentioned at various points the idea that certain aspects of mind, such as intentionality, the emotions and consciousness, as well as possibly rationality itself, might in fact be essentially biologically based. This is only a possibility, of course, but if it proves to be at all along the right lines, then the ancient and scholastic view that the soul is the form of a living body may not be far from correct. Perhaps, that is, there is some truth after all in Aquinas's view that 'it is not to the detriment of the soul that it is united to a body, but for the perfection of its nature' (*Quaestio disputata de anima*, 2nd article in reply to 14th objection).

Further reading

A very accessible and fascinating account of the rise of naturalism, under the influence of behaviourist psychology, neurophysiology and computing, is Lyons (2001). For good critical accounts of B.F. Skinner's scientific behaviourism, see Dennett's 'Skinner skinned', in *Brainstorms* (1978), and chapter four of Owen Flanagan's *The Science of the Mind* (1991). Readings on other types of behaviourism can be found in the further reading for Chapter 3. One of the best and most accessible philosophical introductions to the computational theory of mind is Tim Crane's *The Mechanical Mind* (2003). See also John Haugland's excellent *Artificial Intelligence: The Very Idea* (1985). A succinct introduction to cognitive science, from a less philosophical and more scientific perspective, and which has influenced the penultimate section of this chapter, is Paul Thagard's *Mind* (1996). Steven Pinker's *How the Mind Works* (1998) is a popular defence of the synthesis of the computational theory of mind with evolutionary psychology (what used to be called 'sociobiology'), written by a cognitive psychologist who specializes in language and vision. For a succinct introduction to connectionism (parallel distributed processing), as well as to related issues in the philosophy of mind, see Paul Churchland's *Matter and Consciousness* (1988). Andy Clark's *Associative Engines* (1993) explores the relation between Fodorian computational views, connectionism and 'folk psychology'. Classic and recent essays in cognitive science can be found in Robert Cummins and Denise Dellarosa Cummins, eds, *Minds, Brains and Computers* (2000). Howard Gardner provides the definitive history of cognitive science in his *The Mind's New Science. A History of the Cognitive Revolution* (1987). Probably the best single-volume reference work on cognitive science is *The MIT Encyclopaedia of the Cognitive Sciences*, edited by Robert A. Wilson and Frank A. Keil. John (1999). Searle's vigorous critique of that branch of cognitive science known as 'artificial intelligence' or 'AI' for short, *Minds, Brains and Science* (1984), is a must read. Huber Dreyfus's *What Computers* Still *Can't Do* (1992) is another famous critique of AI. For the simulation theory/theory-theory debate see the two volumes of philosophical and psychological essays edited by Martin Davies and Tony Stone: *Folk Psychology: The Theory of Mind Debate* and *Mental Simulation: Evaluations and Applications* (both 1995). Wilfred Sellars's discussion of the theoretical nature of commonsense psychology can be found in his classic 1956 essay 'Empiricism and the Philosophy of Mind', reprinted in Sellars (1997), which includes an introduction by Richard Rorty and a study guide by Robert Brandom. Essays on eliminativism can be found in both Rosenthal's (1991) and Lycan's (1999) readers. For the Fodorian presentation of the computational theory of mind that I have drawn on here, see Fodor's *Psychosemantics. The Problem of Meaning in the Philosophy of Mind* (1987), in which he also presents this theory of representational content, the latter of which is further refined in his *A Theory of Content and Other Essays* (1990). For the contrasting view, sometimes called 'functional role semantics', see Ned Block's, 'Advertisement of a semantics for psychology' (1986). Fodor's latest and more explicitly pessimistic views on the computational theory of mind can be found in his *The Mind Doesn't Work That Way* (2000), which is an attack on Pinker's optimism. Fodor's writings are an odd combination of a casual down-to-earth style with a forbiddingly technical vocabulary. Before tackling them, it is worth reading two of his less technical and fairly accessible pieces: 'The Big Idea', in the *Times Literary Supplement* (1992), and his intellectual self-profile 'Fodor, Jerry' in *The Blackwell Companion to the Philosophy of Mind*, ed. Samuel Guttenplan (1994). Georges Rey's *Contemporary Philosophy of Mind* (1997) is a good introduction to philosophy of mind from a cognitive science perspective and offers a fairly accessible defence of Fodor's computational theory of mind. Daniel Dennett's 'A cure for the common cold', in his *Brainstorms* (1978), is an important early critique of Fodor's 'language of thought' hypothesis. For Richard Rorty's iconoclastic and wide-angle view of twentieth-century philosophy of mind, see his essay 'Contemporary philosophy of mind' (1982) and Dennett's response 'Comments on Rorty' (1982).

Glossary

A posteriori something is knowable a posteriori if it can be known on the basis of some particular experience of some particular course of events in the world. E.g. the proposition 'There are over a thousand species of beetle' is knowable a posteriori.

A priori something is knowable a priori if it can be known independently of any experience of any course of events in the world. E.g. the proposition '9 +0=9' is knowable a priori.

Abduction (aka inference to the best explanation) reasoning from a premise about some body of data to a conclusion that is the best explanation of the data. E.g. from the existence of certain kinds of primitive artefacts, archaeologists infer that early humans hunted animals. In abduction, the truth of the premises does not guarantee the truth of the conclusion. See also **deduction** and **induction**.

Aristotelianism doctrines associated with the ancient Greek philosopher Aristotle, such as **hylomorphism**.

Attitude a mental state with content. When the content in question is propositional, the attitude is known as a *propositional attitude*. See **content**.

Attribute in Descartes's philosophy, an attribute is the defining property of a substance. Thought is the 'principal attribute' of mind and extension is the 'principal attribute' of matter. See **substance** and **mode**.

Automaton a creature that has no conscious experience.

Behaviourism in philosophy, the view that mental states can be analysed in terms of behaviour (this is *logical* or *analytical* behaviourism). In psychology, the view that the study of the mind must restrict itself to behaviour (this is *scientific* or *methodological* behaviourism). Contrast **cognitivism**.

Cartesianism doctrines associated with Descartes, in particular **dualism** and **mechanism** and their implications.

Category mistake the mistake of assigning something to a category to which it does not belong. E.g. to say that numbers are coloured would be to commit a category mistake because numbers are not the kinds of thing that can be coloured.

Cognitivism (aka mentalism) the view, opposed to **behaviourism**, that psychology must make reference to internal and causally efficacious mental states and processes in order to explain cognition and intelligent behaviour.

Commonsense psychology (aka folk psychology) our everyday framework of mental concepts that we employ in explaining, predicting and generally making intelligible the thoughts and behaviour of intelligent creatures. See also **theory theory** and **simulation theory**.

Computational process the manipulation of symbols solely on the basis of their **syntactic properties** according to a fixed set of rules.

Content (aka intentional content or representational content) a mental state has content when it has **intentionality**. Propositional content is content specified by a proposition and thus can be assessed as true or false. The belief that Shakespeare wrote *Othello* has propositional content; but Iago's hatred of Othello does not. See also **attitude**.

Contingent truth a truth that can possibly be false. E.g. the statement 'The earth has one moon' is contingently true because it might have had two or more or no moons. Contrasted with **necessary truth**.

Deduction reasoning in which the truth of the premises guarantees the truth of the conclusion; i.e., reasoning in which it is impossible for the premises to be true and the conclusion false. See also **abduction** and **induction**.

Deviant an imaginary replica of a human being who behaves just like we do, but who has different conscious experiences from us, for example, feels tickling sensations instead of pain when burned with fire.

Disposition a propensity to exhibit or manifest a particular reaction in certain circumstances. Solubility is a disposition. Some mental states, for example, belief and intention, appear to be dispositions.

Dualism *substance dualism* is the view that there are two fundamentally distinct kinds of substances, such as mind and body in Descartes's philosophy. There are other kinds of dualism, such as *property dualism*, the view that there are two kinds of properties in the world, for example, mental and physical properties. Some philosophers uphold property dualism but reject substance dualism.

Eliminativism (in the philosophy of mind) the view that **commonsense psychology** is a false empirical theory of cognition and the causes of intelligent behaviour.

Form see **matter and form**.

Functionalism the view that types of mental states – beliefs, desires, pains, etc. – are characterized by their causal roles in the overall mental life of a creature. Functionalists usually uphold the **multiple realizability** of the mental.

Hylomorphism in Aristotelian philosophy, the view that all change is to be accounted for in terms of **matter** (Greek *hyle*) **and form** (Greek *morphe*). Contrast **mechanism**.

Identity theory generally, the view that mental phenomena are identical with physical phenomena. The *type identity theory* asserts that for every kind of mental state (pain, e.g.) there will correspond a certain physical kind. The token identity theory asserts, more weakly, that every instance of a mental kind (e.g. the headache I am having right now) is identical with an instance of some or other physical kind.

Induction reasoning from a premise about some observed cases to a conclusion about some unobserved cases. E.g. inferring from the fact that all of the many swans you have observed have been white to the conclusion that the next one you see will be too. In induction the truth of the premise does not guarantee the truth of the conclusion. See also **abduction** and **deduction**.

Intentionality that aspect of the mind by which it is directed at or about something. See also **attitude** and **content**.

Language of thought (aka mentalese) a symbolic code, consisting of representations with **semantic** and **syntactic properties**, hypothesized as the medium in which thinking takes place.

Materialism originally, the view that everything is made of matter. Now often used as a synonym for *physicalism*, the view that everything is made up of whatever the true and completed science of physics says there is. Some forms of physicalism state that all properties are physical properties, i.e. that all properties are identical with the properties of physics, and thus deny *property dualism*. See **dualism**.

Matter and form in Aristotelian philosophy, there are two aspects to every individual thing: its *matter*, which is the stuff out of which it is made, and its *form*, which is the distinctive way the matter is structured or arranged, or the way it functions, and which makes it the kind of thing that it is.

Mechanism the view, associated especially with certain philosophers and scientists in the seventeenth century, which is opposed to Aristotelian **hylomorphism**, that all change in the universe is to be explained, using mathematical concepts, in terms of the motion of bodies in contact with one another.

Mode in Descartes's philosophy, a modification or change in either in the attribute of thought or the attribute of extension. Being square is a mode of extension; seeing is a mode of thought. See **attribute** and **substance**.

Multiple realizability (aka variable realizability) the idea, associated with **functionalism**, that mental states can be embodied or incarnated in diverse types of media, such as neurons, silicon chips, etc.

Naturalism (in philosophy of mind) *methodological naturalism* is the view that the mind should be studied using scientific methods. There are other forms of naturalism, some of which equate naturalism with some form of **physicalism**.

Necessary truth a truth that cannot possibly be false. E.g., the statement that all triangles have three sides is necessarily true because it is impossible for there to be a triangle that does not have three sides. Contrasted with **contingent truth**.

Physicalism See **materialism**.

Problem of other minds the philosophical problem of whether we can know that others have minds and/or what their minds are like.

Rational soul (aka intellectual soul) in Aristotelian philosophy, that part of the soul responsible for reasoning and judging. See also **sensitive** and **vegetative soul**.

Semantic properties properties of representations that relate them to the world, such as the fact that the word 'Descartes' designates Descartes and that the sentence 'Descartes was a mathematician' refers to the state of affairs of Descartes's being a mathematician. Contrast **syntactic properties**. See also **language of thought**.

Sensitive soul in Aristotelian philosophy, that part of the soul responsible for sensation, perception, locomotion and emotion. See also **rational** and **vegetative soul**.

Simulation theory the view that the practice of **commonsense psychology** involves imaginatively projecting oneself into another person's perspective.

Soul in Aristotelian philosophy, as opposed to its theological sense, the soul is the **form** of a living body, which is responsible for its various biological and cognitive functions and activities. See **rational, sensitive** and **vegetative soul**.

Substance in Descartes's philosophy, something that does not depend on anything but God for its existence. There are two kinds of substance (excluding God): mind and matter. See **attribute** and **mode**.

Syntactic properties the formal or structural properties of representations, such as the shapes or order of physical symbols. Contrast **semantic properties**. See also **language of thought**.

Theory theory the view that **commonsense psychology** is like a scientific theory, in the sense of being a conceptual framework employed to explain, predict and make intelligible the behaviour of intelligent creatures. See also **simulation theory**.

Thomism doctrines associated with St Thomas Aquinas.

Type/token distinction types are *kinds* and tokens are *instances* of kinds. My neighbour and I might each own different token cars, which are of the same type (i.e., they are the same make, model and year).

Vegetative soul (aka nutritive soul) in Aristotelian philosophy, that part of the soul responsible for growth, nutrition and reproduction. See also **rational** and **sensitive soul**.

Bibliography

ALANEN, L. (2003) *Descartes's Concept of Mind,* Cambridge, Mass., Harvard University Press.

ANTONY, L. and HORNSTEIN, N. (eds) (2003) *Chomsky and his Critics*, Oxford, Blackwell.

ARMSTRONG, D.M. (1968) *A Materialist Theory of the Mind*, London, Routledge and Kegan Paul.

ARMSTRONG, D.M. (1981) 'The nature of mind', in his *The Nature of Mind*, Brighton, Harvester.

ARMSTRONG, D.M. and MALCOLM, N. (1984) *Consciousness and Causality*, Oxford, Blackwell.

AYERS, M. (1991) *Locke: Epistemology and Ontology,* London, Routledge.

BAKER, G. and MORRIS, K.J. (1996) *Descartes's Dualism*, Oxford, Blackwell.

BARNES, J. (ed.) (1995) *The Cambridge Companion to Aristotle*, Cambridge, Cambridge University Press.

BLOCK, N. (ed.) (1980) *Readings in Philosophy of Psychology*, vol. 1, Cambridge, Mass., Harvard University Press.

BLOCK, N. (1986) 'Advertisement of a semantics for psychology', *Midwest Studies in Philosophy*, 10.

BLOOM, H. (1997) *Omens of the Millennium,* Riverhead Books.

BRADDON-MITCHELL, D. and JACKSON, F. (1996) *Philosophy of Mind and Cognition*, Oxford, Blackwell.

BUDD, M. (1989) *Wittgenstein's Philosophy of Psychology*, London, Routledge.

CHAPPELL, V. (ed.) (1998) *Locke*, Oxford Readings in Philosophy, Oxford, Oxford University Press.

CHOMSKY, N. (1988) *Language and Problems of Knowledge*, Cambridge, Mass., MIT Press.

CHOMSKY, N. (2000) *New Horizons in the Study of Language and Mind*, Cambridge, Cambridge University Press.

CLARK, A. (1993) *Associative Engines*, Cambridge, Mass., MIT Press.

CHURCHLAND, P. (1988) *Matter and Consciousness*, Cambridge, Mass., MIT Press.

COTTINGHAM, J. (1986), *Descartes*, Oxford, Blackwell.

COTTINGHAM, J. (ed.) (1992) *The Cambridge Companion to Descartes*, Cambridge, Cambridge University Press.

COTTINGHAM, J. (ed.) (1998), *Descartes*, Oxford Readings in Philosophy, Oxford, Oxford University Press.

CRANE, T. (2001) *The Elements of Mind,* Oxford, Oxford University Press.

CRANE, T. (2003) *The Mechanical Mind*, 2nd edn, London, Routledge.

CRANE, T. and PATTERSON, S. (eds) (2000) *History of the Mind–Body Problem*, London, Routledge.

CUMMINS, R. and DELLAROSA CUMMINS, D. (eds) (2000) *Minds, Brains and Computers*, Oxford, Blackwell.

DAMASIO, A. (1994) *Descartes's Error,* New York, Grosset/Putnam.

DAVIDSON, D. (1980) 'Mental events', in his *Essays on Actions and Events*, Oxford, Clarendon (first published 1970).

DAVIES, M. and STONE, T. (1995) *Folk Psychology: The Theory of Mind Debate*, Oxford, Blackwell.

DAVIES, M. and STONE, T. (1995) *Mental Simulation: Evaluations and Applications,* Oxford, Blackwell.

DENNETT, D. (1978) *Brainstorms*, Cambridge, Mass., MIT Press.

DENNETT, D. (1982) 'Comments on Rorty', *Synthese*, 53, 249–356.

DENNETT, D. (1987) *The Intentional Stance*, Cambridge, Mass., MIT Press.

DENNETT, D. (1991) *Consciousness Explained*, Boston, Little, Brown and Co.

DENNETT, D. (1996) *Kinds of Minds*, New York, Basic Books.

DESCARTES, R. (1985) *The Philosophical Writings of Descartes*, vols I–III, edited by Cottingham, J., Stoothoff, R., Murdoch, D. and Kenny, A., Cambridge, Cambridge University Press

DREYFUS, H. (1992) *What Computers* Still *Can't Do*, Cambridge, Mass., MIT Press.

FLANAGAN, O. (1991) *The Science of the Mind*, 2nd edn, Cambridge, Mass., MIT Press.

FLOYD, J. and SHIEH, S. (eds) (2001) *Future Pasts. The Analytic Tradition in Twentieth-century Philosophy*, New York, Oxford University Press.

FODOR, J. (1968) *Psychological Explanation*, New York, Random House.

FODOR, J. (1975) *The Language of Thought*, Cambridge, Mass., Harvard.

FODOR, J. (1981) 'The mind–body problem', *Scientific American*, Jan., 114–23.

FODOR, J. (1987) *Psychosemantics: The Problem of Meaning in the Philosophy of Mind*, Cambridge, Mass., MIT Press.

FODOR, J. (1990) *A Theory of Content and Other Essays,* Cambridge, Mass., MIT Press.

FODOR, J. (1992) 'The Big Idea', *The Times Literary Supplement,* 3 July, 5–7.

FODOR, J. (1994) 'Fodor, Jerry' in Guttenplan (1994), pp.292–300.

FODOR, J. (2000) *The Mind Doesn't Work That Way*, Cambridge, Mass., MIT Press.

GARBER, D. and AYERS, M. (eds) (1998) *Cambridge History of Seventeenth-century Philosophy*, Cambridge, Cambridge University Press.

GARDNER, H. (1987) *The Mind's New Science. A History of the Cognitive Revolution*, New York, Basic Books.

GEACH, P. (1957) *Mental Acts. Their Content and their Objects*, London, Routledge and Kegan Paul.

GUTTENPLAN, S. (ed.) (1994) *The Blackwell Companion to the Philosophy of Mind,* Oxford, Blackwell.

GUTTENPLAN, S. (2000) *Mind's Landscape*, Oxford, Blackwell.

HATFIELD, G. (2001) 'Epistemology and science in the image of modern philosophy: Rorty on Descartes and Locke', in Floyd and Shieh (2001), pp.393–413.

HAUGLAND, J. (1985) *Artificial Intelligence: The Very Idea*, Cambridge Mass., MIT Press.

HEMPEL, C. (1980) 'The logical analysis of psychology', in Block (1980).

HOBBES, T. (1996) *Leviathan*, Oxford, Oxford University Press (first published 1651).

HUME, D. (1978) *A Treatise of Human Nature*, P.H. Nidditch, ed., Oxford, Clarendon Press (first published 1739–40).

JAMES, S. (1997) *Passion and Action. The Emotions in Seventeenth-century Philosophy,* Cambridge, Cambridge University Press.

JAMES, W. (1983) *The Principles of Psychology*, Cambridge, Mass., Harvard University Press (first published 1890).

JONES, W.T. (1969) *A History of Western Philosophy. Vol III: Hobbes to Hume,* 2nd edn, San Diego, Harcourt, Brace, Jovanovich.

KIM, J. (1996) *Philosophy of Mind*, Oxford, West View Press.

KOHLER, W. (1925) *The Mentality of Apes*, London, Routledge and Kegan Paul.

KRETZMAN, N. and STUMP, E. (eds) (1993) *The Cambridge Companion to Aquinas*, Cambridge, Cambridge University Press.

LOCKE, J. (1975) *An Essay Concerning Human Understanding,* P.H. Nidditch, ed., Oxford, Clarendon Press (first published 1689).

LOCKE, J. (1997) *An Essay Concerning Human Understanding,* R. Woolhouse, ed., Harmondsworth, Penguin (first published 1689).

LOWE, E.J. (1995) *Locke on Human Understanding,* London, Routledge.

LOWE, E.J. (2000) *An Introduction to the Philosophy of Mind,* Cambridge, Cambridge University Press.

LYCAN, W. (ed.) (1999) *Mind and Cognition*, 2nd edn, Oxford, Blackwell (1st edn 1990).

LYONS, W. (ed.) (1995) *Modern Philosophy of Mind*, London, Everyman.

LYONS, W. (2001) *Matters of Mind*, Edinburgh, Edinburgh University Press.

MACDONALD, P.S. (2003) *History of the Concept of Mind. Speculations about Soul, Mind and Spirit from Homer to Hume*, Aldershot, Ashgate.

O'SHAUGHNESSY, B. (2000) *Consciousness and the World*, Oxford, Clarendon Press.

PINKER, S. (1998) *How the Mind Works*, Harmondsworth, Penguin.

PLACE, U.T. (1999) 'Is consciousness a brain process?', in Lycan (1999), pp.14–19 (first published 1956).

RAMACHANDRAN, V.S. (2003) *The Emerging Mind*, London, Profile Books.

RAMACHANDRAN, V.S. and BLAKESLEE, S. (1998) *Phantoms in the Brain*, London, Fourth Estate.

REY, G. (1997) *Contemporary Philosophy of Mind*, Oxford, Blackwell.

RORTY, R. (1979) *Philosophy and the Mirror of Mature*, Princeton, New Jersey, Princeton University Press.

RORTY, R. (1982) 'Contemporary philosophy of mind', *Synthese*, 53, 323–48.

ROSENTHAL, D. (ed.) (1991) *The Nature of Mind*, Oxford, Oxford University Press.

ROZEMOND, M. (1998) *Descartes's Dualism*, Cambridge, Mass., Harvard University Press.

RYLE, G. (1979) *On Thinking*, Oxford, Blackwell.

RYLE, G. (2000) *Concept of Mind,* Harmondsworth, Penguin (first published 1949).

SACKS, O. (1986) *The Man Who Mistook His Wife for a Hat*, Picador.

SEARLE, J. (1984) *Minds, Brains and Science*, Cambridge, Mass., Harvard.

SEARLE, J. (1992) *The Rediscovery of the Mind*, Cambridge, Mass., MIT Press.

SELLARS, W. (1997) *Empiricism and the Philosophy of Mind,* Cambridge, Mass., Harvard University Press (first published 1956).

SMART, J.J.C. (1991) 'Sensations and brain processes', in Rosenthal (1991), pp.169–76..(first published 1959).

STRAWSON, G. (1994) *Mental Reality*, Cambridge, Mass., MIT Press.

STROUD, B. (2000) *The Quest for Reality. Subjectivism and the Metaphysics of Colour*, New York, Oxford University Press.

THAGARD, P. (1996) *Mind. Introduction to Cognitive Science*, Cambridge, Mass., MIT Press.

WILLIAMS, B. (1978) *Descartes, The Project of Pure Enquiry*, Harmondsworth, Penguin.

WILSON, M . (1978) *Descartes*, London, Routledge and Kegan Paul.

WILSON, M. (1999) *Ideas and Mechanism*, Princeton, Princeton University Press.

WILSON, R.A. and KEIL, F.A. (eds) (1999) *The MIT Encyclopaedia of the Cognitive Sciences*, Cambridge, Mass., MIT Press.

WITTGENSTEIN, L. (1953) *Philosophical Investigations,* trans. G.E.M. Anscombe, Oxford, Blackwell.

WITTGENSTEIN, L. (1967) *Zettel*, trans. G.E.M. Anscombe, Oxford, Blackwell.

YOLTON, J. (1983) *Thinking Matter. Materialism in Eighteenth-century Britain*, Minneapolis, University of Minnesota Press.

READINGS

READING 1

Consciousness and Life

Gareth B. Matthews

Source: Matthews, Gareth B. (1977) 'Consciousness and life', *Philosophy*, LII, 199, 13–26; reprinted in Rosenthal, David M. (ed.) (1991) *The Nature of Mind*, Oxford, Oxford University Press, pp.63–70.

[I]

In L. Frank Baum's story, *Ozma of Oz*, which is a sequel to Baum's much more famous story, *The Wonderful Wizard of Oz*, Dorothy and her companion come upon a wound-down mechanical man bearing a label on which are printed the following words:

> Smith and Tinkers's
> Patent Double-Action, Extra-Responsive, Thought-Creating
> Perfect-Talking
> MECHANICAL MAN
> Fitted with out Special Clock-Work Attachment
> Thinks, Speaks, Acts, and Does Everything but Live
>
> (*Ozma of Oz*, Chicago, 1907, p.43)

As Dorothy and her companion are made to discover when they wind up this man ('Tik-Tok' is his name), he is indeed capable of doing all the things of which his label boasts – acting, speaking and even thinking. But as Tik-Tok himself insists, and no one in the story casts doubt on the matter, he is not alive.

Dorothy and her companion learn from the instructions that to make Tik-Tok think they are to wind under one of his arms, to make him talk they are to wind under the other, and to make him move about they are to wind in the middle of his back.

'Which shall we do first?' asks Dorothy. 'Wind up his think,' advises her companion. So she does. 'I don't see anything different,' says Dorothy after a moment's wait. 'Of course not,' explains her companion. 'He's just thinking; if you want to know *what* he's thinking, wind up his talk.' So Dorothy does. 'T-h-a-n-k y-o-u v-e-r-y m-u-c-h,' says Tik-Tok somewhat rustily.

Dorothy contrasts the case of Tik-Tok, who is incapable of living, with that of Nick Chopper, the much more famous tin man of *The Wonderful Wizard of Oz*. In *Ozma of Oz* Dorothy puts the contrast this way:

> Once... I knew a man made out of tin, who was a woodman named Nick Chopper. But he was live as we are, 'cause he was born a real man, and got his tin body a little at a time – first a leg and then a finger and then an ear – for the reason that he had so many accidents with his axe, and cut himself up in a very careless manner (p.42).

Dorothy's account is slightly inaccurate, as checked against the original story. Nick did not, according to his own account of the matter in *The Wonderful Wizard of Oz*, lose parts of his original body through carelessness, but rather because of a wicked witch who cast a spell on his axe.

But the really important point is that Nick started out as a creature of flesh and bones and ended up as a creature of tin by the gradual, piece-by-piece replacement of each limb and gross segment of his body.

The story of Nick's life is a modern variant of the ancient tale of the ship of Theseus, the boards of which were replaced one plank at a time. The puzzle with Nick, as with the ship, is to say whether the original entity persists through the gradual replacement of each of its parts and, if it does not, to say just at what point in the proceedings it ceases to exist.

Nick's story adds two new and conceptually significant features to the old tale of the ship of Theseus. First, the replacement pieces are, in his case, of a different material from the parts they replace. Each time he gets a tin replacement for a fleshy original. Just how and why the material might be important to the question of persistence through time is not easy to say. To gain some appreciation for how 'not easy' it is one need only have a look at Aristotle's tortured efforts in *Metaphysics* Z10 to say whether, and if so, in what way, matter might belong to the form or essence or definition of a thing. The issues involved in this question become more pressing as we today become more and more clever at replacing parts of human bodies with fabricated substitutes.

The second new feature in Nick's story of gradual transformation is the fact that *he* tells the story as the story of *his* life. He seems able to remember being the creature of flesh and bones on whose axe the wicked witch cast a spell. In the case of persons, memory has long been a favourite candidate for a criterion of identity.

None of these considerations applies to Tik-Tok. He seems to have been fashioned in a tinker's shop. He is not the product of the gradual transformation of a living thing. He seems to be, as his label suggests, quite incapable of living.

One might want to draw a distinction between thinking and consciousness, to allow, for example, that a computer might be capable of thought, but not of consciousness. In the story, however, no such distinction is drawn; Tik-Tok is treated as a conscious being. So, if the story is coherent, neither

(1) Tik-Tok thinks

nor even

(2) Tik-Tok is conscious

entails

(3) Tik-Tok is alive.

That is, if the story is coherent there is nothing incoherent or self-contradictory about the claim that, while (1) and (2) are true, (3) is false.

In a paper called 'Robots: Machines or Artificially Created Life?' Hilary Putnam reports, as follows, an (as he says) 'ingenious argument', which he attributes to Paul Ziff:

> Ziff wishes to show that it is false that [the robot] Oscar is conscious. He begins with the undoubted fact that if Oscar is not alive he cannot be conscious. Thus, given the semantical connection between 'alive' and 'conscious' in English, it is enough to show that Oscar is not *alive*. Now, Ziff argues, when we wish to tell whether or not something is alive, we do *not* go by its *behaviour*. Even if a thing looks like a flower, grows in my garden like a flower, etc., if I find upon taking it apart that it consists of gears and wheels and miniaturized furnaces and vacuum tubes and so on, I say 'What a clever mechanism', not 'What an unusual plant'. It

> is *structure,* not *behaviour* that determines whether or not something is alive; and it is a violation of the semantical rules of our language to say of anything that is clearly a mechanism that it is 'alive'.[1]

I shall suppose that the talk of semantical rules at the end of this quotation can be expressed by saying that 'x is a mechanism' entails '~ (x is alive)'. It would then be Ziff's claim (as reported by Putnam) that

(4) Tik-Tok is a mechanism

which, one might say, is proclaimed on Tik-Tok's label, entails

(3′) Tik-Tok is not alive

and (3′) in turn entails

(2′) Tik-Tok is not conscious.

If we assume again that neither Putnam or Ziff intends to make any crucial distinction between being conscious and thinking, we could as well say that (3′) entails

(1′) Tik-Tok does not think.

The upshot is that, according to Ziff, Tik-Tok's label would be self-contradictory.

For any of this to be at all plausible 'mechanism' must be understood in a rather hard-headed way, so than an expression such as 'the mechanisms of mind' would have to be metaphorical and so that in its literal use 'x is a mechanism' would entail that x operates on mechanical principles.

Ziff's reasoning (or anyway, the reasoning Putnam attributes to Ziff) is very traditional. One feels like saying that it is very Aristotelian. But there are good reasons for being cautious about saying that. For one thing, there seems not be a good equivalent in Aristotle's Greek for the word 'conscious' and its cognates.[2] This apparent lack is not trivial; it has, in part, to do with the very separation of consciousness from life and bodily function that is under discussion.

For another thing, one might be worried about whether Aristotle had a concept of mechanism like ours. Evidence that he did is, perhaps, to be found in his discussion of mechanical toys as models for animal movement in *De*

Motu Animalium (701b1) and as models for reproduction in *De Generation Animalium* (734b10).

Then there are those hesitations about whether thinking, even among mortal things, requires a body (at, e.g. 403a6, 408b18, 413a6, 413b24) – hesitations resolved, perhaps, by Aristotle's doctrine that thinking requires an image, a phantasm (431a16, 431b2, 432a8, 432a13).

Certainly Aristotle is willing to suppose that eternal things think; in *Metaphysics* A7 he tells us that the prime mover does. But then it also lives – not in the way you and I do, but in a way appropriate to itself. So if Aristotle were to conclude that Tik-Tok thinks, there is reason to suppose he would also conclude that Tik-Tok lives.

The discussions of toys I referred to earlier suggest that Aristotle would not be willing to call Tik-Tok, or Ziff's mechanical flower, alive. So perhaps it is fair to connect Aristotle with Ziff's reasoning. With respect to astronomy and theology, Ziff and Aristotle might disagree about what things think and therefore about what things are alive; but perhaps they are quite close on the connection between thinking and living and the separation between being a mechanism and either thinking or living.

By contrast, explicitly drawn contrast, Descartes sought to break the conceptual connection between being conscious and being alive. Here is a revealing comment from Descartes' *Reply to Objections V:*

> ...because probably men in the earliest times did not distinguish in us that principle in virtue of which we are nourished, grow, and perform all those operations which are common to us with the brutes apart from any thought, from that by which we think, they called both by the single name *soul*... But I, perceiving that the principle by which we are nourished is wholly distinct from that by means of which we think, have declared that the name *soul* when used for both is equivocal ... I consider the mind not as part of the soul, but as the whole of that soul which thinks.[3]

Descartes makes clear elsewhere that he wants to give an account of something's being alive in terms of its having in it warm blood. Here is one such passage:

> ...I would not wish to say that motion is the soul of brutes... I would prefer to say with the Bible (Deuteronomy, xii, 23, 'Only be sure that you eat not the blood; for the blood is the life; and you may not eat the life with the flesh') that blood is their

> soul; for blood is a fluid in rapid movement, and its more rarefied parts are called spirits. It is these which move the whole machine of the body as they flow from the arteries through the brain into the nerves and muscles.[4]

The mind, of course, has no blood in it (none, at least, in the relevant way, or perhaps in the relevant sense of 'in') and therefore is not alive. Yet the mind thinks, is conscious. Thus it does not follow from the fact that something is conscious that it is alive. Indeed, although the person made up of body and mind can presumably both be said to be alive and to be conscious, Descartes understands the person to be alive because the body is alive and conscious because the mind is conscious.

There is another way in which Descartes opposed the Ziffian argument. Descartes understands the corporeal soul to be a purely mechanical principle. He thus refuses to accept the alleged distinction between mechanisms and living organisms. The following quotation from Descartes' *Treatise of Man* expresses clearly Descartes' thesis that the living human body is a machine and operates on mechanical principles no different from those on which clocks operate:

> I desire you to consider, further, that all the functions that I have attributed to this machine, such as (a) the digestion of food; (b) the beating of the heart and arteries; (c) the nourishment and growth of the members; (d) respiration; (e) waking and sleeping; (f) the reception of the external sense organs of light, sounds, smells, tastes, heat, and other such qualities; (g) the imprinting of the ideas of these qualities in the organ of common sense and imagination; (h) the retention or imprint of these ideas in the memory; (i) the internal movements of the appetites and passions; and finally (j), the external movement of all the members that so properly follow both the actions of objects presented to the senses and the passions and impressions which are entitled in the memory – I desire you to consider, I say, that these functions imitate those of a real man as perfectly as possible and that they follow naturally in this machine entirely from the disposition of the organs – no more nor less than do the movements of a clock or other automation, from the arrangement of its counterweights and wheels. Wherefore it is not necessary, on their account, to conceive of any vegetative or sensitive soul or any other principle of movement and life than its blood and its spirits, agitated by the heat of the fire which burns continually in its heart and which is of no other nature than all those fires that occur in inanimate bodies.[5]

Thus according to Descartes

(4) Tik-Tok is a mechanism

fails to entail either

(2′) Tik-Tok is not conscious

or

(1′) Tik-Tok does not think

both because it fails to entail

(3′) Tik-Tok is not alive

and because (3′) fails to entail (2′). In other words, Descartes rejected both a traditional connection and a traditional separation. The traditional connection he rejected is that between thinking, or being conscious, and living. He said that they do not really go together at all, except by a mysterious, divinely ordered coincidence. The traditional separation he rejected is the separation of living things and mechanisms; he said that living things are machines of a certain sort.[6] The separation, like the connection, is traditional, though it was not universally accepted, even in the ancient world. Thales, according to Aristotle (*De Anima* 405a19), ascribed soul to magnets. We do not know for sure that he also said magnets are alive. But there is every reason to suppose he accepted the ancient commonplace that whatever has soul is alive. If so, and if a magnet counts as a mechanism, then Thales is a precursor of Descartes in denying the separation between living things and mechanisms.

Still, the ancient world did not, in general, follow Thales in this line of thought. And Descartes certainly gives every evidence that he thought himself something of a radical in conceiving the living human body as a machine. In fact he was so nervous about his radicalism and apprehensive of censure from officialdom that he disguised his claim in the *Treatise of Man* by making it explicitly a claim about a *model* of human physiology. (In other context he was more forthright.[7])

As against Descartes, and in support of a somewhat Aristotelian position, Ziff claims that our language embodies a conceptual connection between being conscious and living and a conceptual incompatibility between being a mechanism and living. His claim is thus that our language remains resolutely anti-Cartesian on these matters.

Putnam, in his critique of the Ziffian argument, affirms the traditional connection between thinking and being alive. He speaks of 'the undoubted fact that if Oscar [the robot; we could substitute Tik-Tok, the Mechanical

Man] is not alive he cannot be conscious' and of the 'semantical connection between "alive" and "conscious"'. But Putnam also shows some sympathy for Descartes' position in that he suspects the distinction between what is alive and what is mechanical is not clear-cut. It might be, he reasons, that some thinking thing, though alive, is yet also mechanical. The sympathy is only very limited. Descartes' claim was not really that you could make a mechanical man that would be alive; his claim was that living bodies *are* machines.

To make out the possibility that some robot might be alive Putman maintains that criteria for life are of two quite different sorts – structural criteria and behavioural criteria. With plants it is, he says, structural criteria that are most important. With animals, or at least with human, or human-like, beings, behavioural criteria come into their own.

Crudely, Putnam's idea is this. Any robot with a programme that matched some reasonably good psychological theory of how people behave would thereby satisfy the behavioural criteria not only for being conscious but also for being alive. If it satisfied the *behavioural* criteria for life; but not the structural criteria, then so much the worse for the structural criteria in that case. It might, for all that, be alive.

What Ziff and Putnam call 'structural criteria' amount, I suppose, to some sort of biochemical definition of 'life'. By contrast the behavioural criteria would seem to belong to the family of functional criteria – digestion/absorption, growth, reproduction, self-motion, sensation/perception, and so on. It would be one thing to use two such basically different sets of criteria to get at roughly the same class of things. It is quite another thing to use one set of criteria for one group of putatively living things and another set for quite a different group. To do that would be, it seems, tantamount to admitting that 'living' means something quite different when it applies to plants, say, from what it means as applied to human beings or human-being-like mechanisms.

Perhaps Putnam thinks that the expressions 'living' and 'alive' are fundamentally equivocal in just such a way. I myself think that the concept of life is complex and rather unclear in a number of ways. But Putnam's talk of two sets of criteria suggests that there are really two different concepts that can be rather neatly marked off from each other, and that our single English word 'alive' equivocally expresses now the one concept and now the other. I, for one, would have to be convinced that that is so.

What I want to concentrate on, however, is not what Putnam contests, but what he concedes, namely, that as our language now stands 'x is conscious' does indeed entail 'x is alive'. Speaking of the corresponding French and Latin words of his day Descartes in effect agrees with Putnam. But what Descartes says is that we had better alter the language so that this entailment no longer holds. As Descartes wanted to use the Latin and French words we render with 'thinks' and 'is conscious' and their cognates there would be no entailment from 'x is conscious' to 'x is alive'. I want to consider now why Descartes thought we ought to talk in this way.

[II]

In *Meditation II* Descartes concludes that he is a thinking thing 'a thing which doubts, understands, affirms, denies, wills, refuses, which also imagines and feels', and that he is *not* 'a collection of members which we call the human body'. Moreover, he presents this double conclusion as a deliberate rejection of the traditional concept of soul.[8]

In the following passage from *Meditation II* Descartes encapsulates the traditional concept of soul as animator in confessing that he once held a belief he now rejects:

> ...I considered that I was nourished, that I walked, that I felt, and that I thought, and I referred all these actions to the soul...[9]

In these words one can recognize the traditional concept of soul as that whereby a human being is nourished, moves, perceives and thinks.

'But what am I', Descartes goes on to ask, 'now that I suppose there is a certain genius which is extremely powerful, and, if I may say so, malicious, who employs all his powers in deceiving me?'

This is a very peculiar question. Descartes does not ask, 'What do I *think* I am, now that I suppose such-and-such?' or 'What am I *justified* in thinking I am, now that I realize so-and-so?' He asks, 'What *am* I now that I suppose I might be deceived in all sorts of diabolical ways?' Descartes seems to suppose that what he is, what, as we might put it, actually belongs to him, is going to be something impervious to the most extravagant doubts he can conjure up. The assumption seems to be that what he is, what really and truly belongs to him, is something that he cannot doubt belongs to him. [...]

Let us return to the narrative in *Meditation II*. Am I then a soul, as souls are traditionally conceived? That is, am I that being whereby my body is nourished, moves, perceives and thinks? Well, replies Descartes, 'If it is so that I have no body it is also true that I can neither walk nor take nourishment'. So I can doubt whether either being able to walk or to take nourishment belongs to me. Thus... neither does belong to me.

Descartes moves on to perception, or sensation. 'But one cannot feel without a body', he reminds himself. Descartes then adds this curious remark:

> ...and besides I have thought I perceived many things during sleep that I recognized in my waking moments as not having been experienced at all.

What does Descartes suppose this remark relevant to?

His idea, I think, is this. There goes with the traditional concept of soul the idea that sensation and perception require a body. Consider, for example, this passage from Aristotle's *De Anima:*

> In most cases it seems that none of the affections, whether active or passive, can exist apart from the body. This applies to anger, courage, desire and sensation generally, though possibly thinking is an exception. But if this too is a kind of imagination, or at least is dependent upon imagination [the alternative Aristotle seems to opt for], even this cannot exist apart from the body.[10]

It is not just that anger, courage, desire, and sensation generally, *as it happens*, turn out not to be manageable without a body. It is rather that a proper account of what these things are will bring in the physiology of anger, courage, desire and sensation. One could say that, using 'sense' (or 'perceive') in a traditional way,

(5) X senses (perceives) something

entails

(6) X has a bodily organ of sensation (perception)

and thus

(7) X has a body (or is a body).

Descartes reasons that if I am going to use 'senses' and 'perceives' in this traditional way, I must say that sensation and perception do not belong to me, for I can doubt that I have a body at all and so I can doubt that I have bodily organs through which I might perceive or sense something. The remark about sleep is meant to give substance to this doubt.

A bit later on in *Meditation II* Descartes gives us a new meaning for 'sentire' ('sense' or 'perceive'). In that new meaning the objectionable entailment does not hold. Here is what he says:

> ...I am the same who feels, that is to say, who perceives certain things, *as by organs of sense,* since in truth I see light, I hear noise, I feel heat. But it will be said that these phenomena are false and that I am dreaming. Let it be so; still it is at least quite certain that it *seems to me* that I see light, that I hear noise and that I feel heat. This cannot be false, *properly speaking* it is what in me is called feeling [*'sentire'*]; and used in *this precise sense* that is no other than thinking [or consciousness] (emphasis added).

This passage makes quite clear that Descartes thought of himself as recommending a way to use the terms for mental acts, or acts of consciousness. He wanted us to use them in such a way that the entailment from (5) to (6) and (7) will not hold – nor will the alleged entailment from (1), or (2), to (3).

In rejecting the traditional concept of soul and denying the traditional connection between consciousness and life Descartes does something much more interesting than simply isolating one function traditionally assigned to soul, namely, thinking, and supposing it to be independent of the rest. Instead he develops a new concept, consciousness, which includes thinking plus the 'inner part' (so to speak) of sensation and perception. Consciousness, conceived in Descartes' way, is the function of a self-transparent agent (the mind) – that is, of an agent whose acts and states are such that it cannot doubt that it has them.

The point is central. Let me have another try at stating it. In giving us the modern concept of mind Descartes does not simply isolate one accepted function of soul and say that a mind is something that does just that. Rather he divides up the functions of the soul in a new way and thinks about them in a new way. He supposed that a mind is a subject that performs a selection of soul-functions such that an entity cannot both perform one of those functions and also doubt that it is performing it. We must (so to speak) 'peel off' from seeing, hearing, tasting etc., the *seeming* to see, to hear, to taste, etc., which is such that one cannot do that and also doubt that one is doing it. The mind is something that does all and only things of that self-revealing sort.

[...]

His idea is that there is a kind of entity, mind, which is self-transparent; for any act it performs and any state it is in, it cannot doubt that it performs that act or is in that state. Furthermore, he, Descartes, is (he supposes) an entity of that kind.

I shall not try to say anything about the vexed question of how Descartes knows he is an entity of that kind, if indeed he does know it, or about what his best argument for proving it might be.[11] For my immediate purpose it is enough to say that Descartes is convinced that he is an entity of such a kind and that others have found it easy to think of themselves as entities of that kind.

The idea that there are entities of this peculiarly self-transparent kind has found wide acceptance in modern thought.

[...]

Subjects of consciousness, according to Descartes, get yoked (albeit temporarily) to living bodies. A human being, as we normally conceive one, is then a mysterious union of mind and body. But each being, so conceived, has both an 'inside' and an 'outside'. The 'inside' is a mind or subject of consciousness, whose acts and states are indubitable to itself. The 'outside' is a body known to the mind or 'inside' only indirectly through quite dubitable inferences from sense impressions.

The picture of human beings as having, in this way, both an 'inside' and an 'outside' is so commonplace, so (as it may seem to us) commonsensical that we find it hard to realize how strikingly modern it is. But to appreciate its modernity one need only cast about for statements of it earlier than Descartes. One does find interesting anticipations of it in Augustine, but not much earlier, and not much between the time of Augustine and that of Descartes. Here is a relevant passage for Augustine's *Contra Academicos;*

> Do not assent to more than that you are convinced that it appears this way to you, and there is no deception; for I do not see how even an Academic can refute a man who says, 'I know that this looks white to me; I know that this sound pleases me; I know that this smells agreeable to me; I know that this tastes sweet to me; I know that this feels cold to me'.... If I am relishing the taste of something, who would be so shameless as to say to me, 'Perhaps you are not tasting, but this is a dream'? Would I stop? Why tasting would give me pleasure even in a dream. Wherefore, no semblance to falsity can confuse what I have said I know (Bk 3, sec. 11, chap.26).

Just a little earlier on in the *Contra Academicos*, in chapter 25, Augustine suggests that one give the name 'world' to whatever impressions one has. Now, he announces triumphantly, this world exists and has whatever character it seems to have. No Academic sceptic can shake my incorrigible knowledge of my own inner world. Augustine's idea in *Contra Academicos* of an 'inner world', impervious to sceptical doubt, is Descartes' idea of the contents of one's mind or consciousness.

Given this Cartesian starting point it becomes a central problem – one familiar to all modern students of philosophy – to justify one's belief that there is an 'outer world' and that this outer world contains living organisms, including, it may be hoped, a living organism that one can identify as one's own body. Thus on Descartes' way of thinking and speaking there is no essential connection between being conscious and being alive, or even between being conscious and having a living body.

If Tik-Tok can carry on an intelligent conversation, there is no good Cartesian reason why he should not be said to be conscious on a basis analogous to that on which you or I might be said to be conscious. He could be a mind in mysterious union with a machine; his machine differs from your machine and mine only in that its physical principle of action is a heavy spring, rather than warm blood.

Suppose the problems of a Cartesian philosophy of mind are in fact as intractable as many people now suppose them to be. When one realizes that these problems arise from a rather deliberate decision by Descartes and his followers to conceive and talk about perception and thinking in a new way, coupled with a deliberate effort to wipe out all suggestion of conceptual incompatibility between being a machine and being alive, it becomes appropriate to ask whether it is a good idea to acquiesce in Descartes' proposal. A full answer to that question would require that one examine the coherence, and, if it is coherent, the usefulness of the idea of a thing whose acts and states are indubitable to itself. But short of giving that full answer one can at least gain perspective on the question by reminding oneself that there is a way of conceiving and discussing these matters, well established in philosophical tradition, in which Tik-Tok's label becomes, as not doubt Frank Baum intended that it should be, a conceptual joke.[12]

Notes

1 'Robots: Machines or Artificially Created Life?', *Journal of Philosophy* 61 (1964), 685–686; reprinted in Hilary Putnam, *Philosophical Papers* (Cambridge, 1975), Vol. 2, 402.

2 For helpful discussions of this question and the whole issue of how Aristotle's philosophy of mind bears on Cartesian ways of thinking see Charles Kahn, 'Sensation and Consciousness in Aristotle's Psychology', *Archiv für Geschichte der Philosophie* 48 (1966), 43–81, and especially Richard Sorabji, 'Body and Soul in Aristotle', *Philosophy* 49 (1974), 63–89.

3 Descartes, *The Philosophical Works,* Haldane and Ross (trans.), (Cambridge, 1931), Vol.2, 210.

4 Letter to Buitendijck (1643), *Philosophical Letters,* A. Kenny (trans), (Oxford, 1970), 146.

5 Descartes, *Treatise of Man,* T. S. Hall (trans), (Cambridge, Mass., 1972), 112–113.

6 What Descartes actually says in the last passage quoted is that the human body is *exactly like* a machine of a certain sort. Elsewhere (e.g. in the passage from his *Description of the Body* quoted by T.S. Hall on pp. 114–115 of his edition of the *Treatise of Man)* he simply says it is a machine.

7 See previous note.

8 I am indebted to Professor G.E.M Anscombe for making clear to me how explicit Descartes' concern with the traditional concept of soul is in *Meditation II.*

9 All translations from *Meditation II* are taken from *The Philosophers Works*, Haldane and Ross (trans.), (Cambridge, 1931), Vol. 1.

10 403a6–10, W.S. Hett translation, Loeb edition.

11 Very helpful on these matters is G.E.M Anscombe, 'The First Person', in *Mind and Language*, S. Guttenplan (ed.), (Oxford, 1975), 45–65.

12 Except for minor alterations the text of this article constitutes the third in a series of eight lectures given under the title, 'The Concept of Soul', in the Divinity School of Cambridge University in the Lent Term, 1976. I am indebted to Professor D.M. MacKinnon, to the other administrators of the Burney Fund and to the members of my wonderfully interdisciplinary audience for the opportunity to develop me ideas on the relevance of the traditional concept of soul to issues of contemporary concern.

READING 2

Descartes' Myth

Gilbert Ryle

Source: Ryle, Gilbert (2000) The Concept of Mind, Harmondsworth, Penguin, pp.13–25. First published 1949, Routledge, www.tandf.co.uk & www.e.bookstore.tandf.co.uk.

1 The official doctrine

There is a doctrine about the nature and place of minds which is so prevalent among theorists and even among laymen that it deserves to be described as the official theory. Most philosophers, psychologists and religious teachers subscribe, with minor reservations, to its main articles and, although they admit certain theoretical difficulties in it, they tend to assume that these can be overcome without serious modifications being made to the architecture of the theory. It will be argued here that the central principles of the doctrine are unsound and conflict with the whole body of what we know about minds when we are not speculating about them.

The official doctrine, which hails chiefly from Descartes, is something like this. With the doubtful exceptions of idiots and infants in arms every human being has both a body and a mind. Some would prefer to say that every human being is both a body and a mind. His body and his mind are ordinarily harnessed together, but after the death of the body his mind may continue to exist and function.

Human bodies are in space and are subject to the mechanical laws which govern all other bodies in space. Bodily processes and states can be inspected by external observers. So a man's bodily life is as much a public affair as are the lives of animals and reptiles and even as the careers of trees, crystals and plants.

But minds are not in space, nor are their operations subject to mechanical laws. The workings of one mind are not witnessable by other observers; its career is private. Only I can take direct cognisance of the states and processes of my own mind. A person therefore lives through two collateral histories, one consisting of what happens in and to his body, the other consisting of what happens in and to his mind. The first is public, the second private. The events in the first history are events in the physical world, those in the second are events in the mental world.

It has been disputed whether a person does or can directly monitor all or only some of the episodes of his own private history; but, according to the official doctrine, of at least some of these episodes he has direct and unchallengeable cognisance. In consciousness, self–consciousness and introspection he is directly and authentically apprised of the present states and operations of his mind. He may have great or small uncertainties about concurrent and adjacent episodes in the physical world, but he can have none about at least part of what is momentarily occupying his mind.

It is customary to express this bifurcation of his two lives and of his two worlds by saying that the things and events which belong to the physical world, including his own body, are external, while the workings of his own mind are internal. This antithesis of outer and inner is of course meant to be construed as a metaphor, since minds, not being in space, could not be described as being spatially inside anything else, or as having things going on spatially inside themselves. But relapses from this good intention are common and theorists are found speculating how stimuli, the physical sources of which are yards or miles outside a person's skin, can generate mental responses inside his skull, or how decisions framed inside his cranium can set going movements of his extremities.

Even when 'inner' and 'outer' are construed as metaphors, the problem how a person's mind and body influence one another is notoriously charged with theoretical difficulties. What the mind wills, the legs, arms and the tongue execute; what affects the ear and the eye has something to do with what the mind perceives; grimaces and smiles betray the mind's moods and bodily castigations lead, it is hoped, to moral improvement. But the actual transactions between the episodes of the private history and those of the public history remain mysterious, since by definition they can belong to neither series. They could not be reported among the happenings described in a person's autobiography of his inner life, but nor could they be reported among those described in someone else's biography of that person's overt career. They can be inspected neither by introspection nor by laboratory experiment. They are theoretical shuttlecocks which are forever being bandied from the physiologist back to the psychologist and from the psychologist back to the physiologist.

Underlying this partly metaphorical representation of the bifurcation of a person's two lives there is a seemingly more profound and philosophical assumption. It is assumed that there are two different kinds of existence or status. What exists or happens may have the status of physical existence, or it may have the status of mental existence. Somewhat as the faces of coins are either heads or tails, or somewhat as living creatures are either male or female, so, it is supposed, some existing is physical existing, other existing is mental existing. It is a necessary feature of what has physical existence that it is in space and time; it is a necessary feature of what has mental existence that is in time but not in space. What has physical existence is composed of matter, or else is a function of matter; what has mental existence consists of consciousness, or else is a function of consciousness.

There is thus a polar opposition between mind and matter, an opposition which is often brought out as follows. Material objects are situated in a common field, known as 'space', and what happens to one body in one part of space is mechanically connected with what happens to other bodies in other parts of space. But mental happenings occur in insulated fields known as 'minds', and there is, apart maybe from telepathy, no direct causal connexion between what happens in one mind and what happens in another. Only through the medium of the public physical world can the mind of one person make a difference to the mind of another. The mind is its own place and in his inner life each of us lives the life of a ghostly Robinson Crusoe. People can see, hear and jolt one another's bodies, but they are irremediably blind and deaf to the workings of one another's minds and inoperative upon them.

What sort of knowledge can be secured of the workings of a mind? On the one side, according to the official theory, a person has direct knowledge of the best imaginable kind of the workings of his own mind. Mental states and processes are (or are normally) conscious states and process, and the consciousness which irradiates them can engender no illusions and leaves the door open for no doubts. A person's present thinkings, feelings and willings, his perceivings, rememberings and imaginings are intrinsically 'phosphorescent'; their existence and their nature are inevitably betrayed to their owner. The inner life is a stream of consciousness of such a sort that it would be absurd to suggest that the mind whose life is that stream might be unaware of what is passing down it.

True, the evidence adduced recently by Freud seems to show that there exist channels tributary to this stream, which run hidden from their owner. People are actuated by impulses the existence of which they vigorously disavow; some of their thoughts differ from the thoughts which they acknowledge; and some of the actions which they think they will to perform they do not really will. They are thoroughly gulled by some of their own hypocrisies and they successfully ignore facts about their mental lives which on the official theory ought to be patent to them. Holders of the official theory tend, however, to maintain that anyhow in normal circumstances a person must be directly and authentically seized of the present state and workings of his own mind.

Besides being currently supplied with these alleged immediate data of consciousness, a person is also generally supposed to be able to exercise from time to time a special kind of perception, namely inner perception, or introspection. He can take a (non-optical) 'look' at what is passing in his mind. Not only can he view and scrutinize a flower through his sense of sight and listen to and discriminate the notes of a bell through his sense of hearing; he can also reflectively or introspectively watch, without any bodily organ of sense, the current episodes of his inner life. This self-observation is also commonly supposed to be immune from illusion, confusion or doubt. A mind's reports of its own affairs have a certainty superior to the best that is possessed by its reports of matters in the physical world. Sense-perceptions can, but consciousness and introspection cannot, be mistaken or confused.

On the other side, one person has no direct access of any sort to the events of the inner life of another. He cannot do better than make problematic inferences from the observed behaviour of the other person's body to the states of mind which, by analogy from his own conduct, he supposes to be signalized by that behaviour. Direct access to the workings of a mind is the privilege of the mind itself; in default of such privileged access, the workings of one mind are inevitably occult to everyone else. For the supposed arguments from bodily movements similar to their own to mental workings similar to their own would lack any possibility of observational corroboration. Not unnaturally, therefore, an adherent of the official theory finds it difficult to resist this consequence of his premisses, that he has no good reason to believe that there do exist minds other than his own. Even if he prefers to believe that to other human bodies there are harnessed minds not unlike his own, he cannot claim to be able to discover their individual characteristics, or the particular things that they undergo and do. Absolute solitude is on this showing the ineluctable destiny of the soul. Only our bodies can meet.

As a necessary corollary of this general scheme there is implicitly prescribed a special way of construing our ordinary concepts of mental powers and operations. The verbs, nouns and adjectives, with which in ordinary life we describe the wits, characters and higher–grade performances of the people with whom we have to do, are required to be construed as signifying special episodes in their secret histories, or else as signifying tendencies for such episodes to occur. When someone is described as knowing, believing or guessing something, as hoping, dreading, intending or shirking something, as designing this or being amused at that, these verbs are supposed to denote the occurrence of specific modifications in his (to us) occult stream of consciousness. Only his own privileged access to this stream in direct awareness and introspection could provide authentic testimony that these mental-conduct verbs were correctly or incorrectly applied. The onlooker, be he teacher, critic, biographer or friend, can never assure himself that his comments have any vestige of truth. Yet it was just because we do in fact all know how to make such comments, make them with general correctness and correct them when they turn out to be confused or mistaken, that philosophers found it necessary to construct their theories of the nature and place of minds. Finding mental-conduct concepts being regularly and effectively used, they properly sought to fix their logical geography. But the logical geography officially recommended would entail that there could be no regular or effective use of these mental-conduct concepts in our descriptions of, and prescriptions for, other people's minds.

2 The absurdity of the official doctrine

Such in outline is the official theory. I shall often speak of it, with deliberate abusiveness, as 'the dogma of the Ghost in the Machine'. I hope to prove that it is entirely false, and false not in detail but in principle. It is not merely an assemblage of particular mistakes. It is one big mistake and a mistake of a special kind. It is, namely, a category-mistake. It represents the facts of mental life as if they belonged to one logical type or category (or range of types or categories), when they actually belong to another. The dogma is therefore a philosopher's myth. In attempting to explode the myth I shall probably be taken to be denying well-known facts about the mental life of human beings, and my plea that I aim at doing nothing more than rectify the logic of mental-conduct concepts will probably be disallowed as mere subterfuge.

I must first indicate what is meant by the phrase 'category-mistake'. This I do in a series of illustrations.

A foreigner visiting Oxford or Cambridge for the first time is shown a number of colleges, libraries, playing fields, museums, scientific departments and administrative offices. He then asks 'But where is the University? I have seen where the members of the Colleges live, where the Registrar works, where the scientists experiment and the rest. But I have not yet seen the University in which reside and work the members of your University'. It has then to be explained to him that the University is not another collateral institution, some ulterior counterpart to the colleges, laboratories and offices which he has seen. The University is just the way in which all that he has already seen is organized. When they are seen and when their coordination is understood, the University has been seen. His mistake lay in his innocent assumption that it was correct to speak of Christ Church, the Bodleian Library, the Ashmolean Museum *and* the University, to speak, that is, as if 'the University' stood for an extra member of the class of which these other units are members. He was mistakenly allocating the University to the same category as that to which the other institutions belong.

The same mistake would be made by a child witnessing the march-past of a division, who, having had pointed out to him such and such battalions, batteries, squadrons, etc., asked when the division was going to appear. He would be supposing that a division was a counterpart to the units already seen, partly similar to them and partly unlike them. He would be shown his mistake by being told that in watching the battalions, batteries and squadrons marching past he had been watching the division marching past. The march-past was not a parade of battalions, batteries, squadrons *and* a division; it was a parade of the battalions, batteries and squadrons *of* a division.

One more illustration. A foreigner watching his first game of cricket learns what are the functions of the bowlers, the batsmen, the fielders, the umpires and the scorers. He then says 'But there is no one left on the field to contribute the famous element of team-spirit. I see who does the bowling, the batting and the wicket-keeping; but I do not see whose role it is to exercise *esprit de corps'*. Once more, it would have to be explained that he was looking for the wrong type of thing. Team-spirit is not another cricketing-operation supplementary to all of the other special tasks. It is, roughly, the keenness with which each of the special tasks is performed, and performing a task keenly is not performing two tasks. Certainly exhibiting team-spirit is not the same thing as bowling or catching, but nor is it a third thing such that we can say that the bowler first bowls *and* then exhibits team-spirit or that a fielder is at a given moment *either* catching *or* displaying *esprit de corps.*

These illustrations of category-mistakes have a common feature which must be noticed. The mistakes were made by people who did not know how to wield the concepts *University, division and team-spirit.* Their puzzles arose from inability to use certain items in the English vocabulary.

The theoretically interesting category-mistakes are those made by people who are perfectly competent to apply concepts, at least in the situations with which they are familiar, but are still liable in their abstract thinking to allocate those concepts to logical types to which they do not belong. An instance of a mistake of this sort would be the following story. A student of politics has learned the main differences between the British, the French, and the American Constitutions, and has learned also the differences and connexions between the Cabinet, Parliament, the various Ministries, the Judicature and the Church of England. But he still became embarrassed when asked questions about the connexions between the Church of England, the Home Office and the British Constitution. For while the Church and the Home Office are institutions, the British Constitution is not another institution in the same sense of that noun. So inter-institutional relations which can be asserted or denied to hold between the Church and the Home Office cannot be asserted or denied to hold between either of them and the British Constitution. 'The British Constitution' is not a term of the same logical type as 'the Home Office' and 'the Church of England'. In a partially similar way, John Doe may be a relative, a friend, an enemy or a stranger to Richard Roe; but he cannot be any of these things to the Average Taxpayer. He knows how to talk sense in certain sorts of discussions about the Average Taxpayer, but he is baffled to say why he could not come across him in the street as he can come across Richard Roe.

It is pertinent to our main subject to notice that, so long as the student of politics continues to think of the British Constitution as a counterpart to the other institutions, he will tend to describe it as a mysteriously occult institution; and so long as John Doe continues to think of the Average Taxpayer as a fellow-citizen, he will tend to think of him as an elusive insubstantial man, a ghost who is everywhere yet nowhere.

My destructive purpose is to show that a family of radical category-mistakes is the source of the double-life theory. The representation of a person as a ghost mysteriously ensconced in a machine derives from this argument. Because, as is true, a person's thinking, feeling and purposive doing cannot be described solely in the idioms of physics, chemistry and physiology, therefore they must be described in counterpart idioms. As the human body is a complex organized unit, so the human mind must be another complex organized unit, thought one made of a different sort of stuff and with a different sort of structure. Or, again, as the human body, like any other parcel of matter, is a field of causes and effects, so the mind must be another field of causes and effects, though not (Heaven be praised) mechanical causes and effects.

3 The origin of the category-mistake

One of the chief intellectual origins of what I have yet to prove to be the Cartesian category-mistake seems to be this. When Galileo showed that his methods of scientific discovery were competent to provide a mechanical theory which should cover every occupant of space, Descartes found in himself two conflicting motives. As a man of scientific genius he could not but endorse the claims of mechanics, yet as a religious and moral man he could not accept, as Hobbes accepted, the discouraging rider to those claims, namely that human nature differs only in degree of complexity from clockwork. The mental could not be just a variety of the mechanical.

He and subsequent philosophers naturally but erroneously availed themselves of the following escape-route. Since mental-conduct words are not to be construed as signifying the occurrence of mechanical processes, they must be construed as signifying the occurrence of non-mechanical processes; since mechanical laws explain movements in space as the effects of other movements in space, other laws must explain some of the non-spatial workings of minds as the effects of other non-spatial workings of minds. The difference between the human behaviours which we describe as intelligent and those which we describe as unintelligent must be a difference in their causation; so, while some movements of human tongues and limbs are the effects of mechanical causes, others must be the effects of non-mechanical causes, i.e. some issue from movements of particles of matter, others from workings of the mind.

The differences between the physical and the mental were thus represented as differences inside the common framework of the categories of 'thing', 'stuff', 'attribute', 'state', 'process', 'change', 'cause' and 'effect'. Minds are things, but different sorts of things from bodies; mental processes are causes and effects, but different sorts of causes and effects from bodily movements. And so on. Somewhat as the foreigner expected the University to be an extra edifice, rather like a college but also considerably different, so the repudiators of mechanism represented minds as extra centres or causal processes, rather like machines but also considerably different from them. Their theory was a para-mechanical hypothesis.

That this assumption was at the heart of the doctrine is shown by the fact that there was from the beginning felt to be a major theoretical difficulty in explaining how minds can influence and be influenced by bodies. How can a mental process, such as willing, cause spatial movements like the movements of the tongue? How can a physical change in the optic nerve have among its effects a mind's perception of a flash of light? This notorious crux by itself shows the logical mould into which Descartes pressed his theory of the mind. It was the self-same mould into which he and Galileo set their mechanics. Still unwittingly adhering to the grammar of mechanics, he tried to avert disaster by describing minds in what was merely an obverse vocabulary. The workings of the minds had to be described by the mere negatives of the specific descriptions given to bodies; they are not in space, they are not motions, they are not modifications of matter, they are not accessible to public observation. Minds are not bits of clockwork, they are just bits of not-clockwork.

As thus represented, minds are not merely ghosts harnessed to machines, they are themselves just spectral machines. Though the human body is an engine, it is not quite an ordinary engine, since some of its workings are governed by another engine inside it – this interior governor-engine being one of a very special sort. It is invisible, inaudible and it has no size or weight. It cannot be taken to bits and the laws it obeys are not those known to ordinary engineers. Nothing is known of how it governs the bodily engine.

A second major crux points the same moral. Since, according to the doctrine, minds belong to the same category as bodies and since bodies are rigidly governed by mechanical laws, it seemed to many theorists to follow that minds must be similarly governed by rigid non-mechanical laws. The physical world is a deterministic system, so the mental world must be a deterministic system. Bodies cannot help the modifications that they undergo, so minds cannot help pursuing the careers fixed for them. *Responsibility, choice, merit* and *demerit* are therefore inapplicable concepts – unless the compromise solution is adopted of saying that the laws governing mental processes, unlike those governing physical processes, have the congenial attribute of being only rather rigid. The problem of the Freedom of the Will was the problem how to reconcile the hypothesis that minds are to be described in terms drawn from the categories of mechanics with the knowledge that higher-grade human conduct is not of a piece with the behaviour of machines.

It is an historical curiosity that it was not noticed that the entire argument was broken-backed. Theorists correctly assumed that any sane man could already recognize the differences between, say, rational and non-rational utterances or between purposive and automatic behaviour. Else there would have been nothing requiring to be salved from mechanism. Yet the explanation given presupposed that one person could in principle never recognize the difference between the rational and the irrational utterances issuing from other human bodies, since he could never get access to the postulated immaterial causes of some of their utterances. Save for the doubtful exception of himself, he could never tell the difference between a man and a Robot. It would have to be conceded, for example, that, for all that we can tell, the inner lives of persons who are classed as idiots or lunatics are as rational as those of anyone else. Perhaps only their overt behaviour is disappointing; that is to say, perhaps 'idiots' are not really idiotic, or 'lunatics' lunatic. Perhaps, too, some of those who are classed as sane are really idiots. According to the theory, external observers could never know how the overt behaviour of others is correlated with their mental powers and processes and so they could never know or even plausibly conjecture whether their applications of mental-conduct concepts to these other people were correct or incorrect. It would then be hazardous or impossible for a man to claim sanity or logical consistency even for himself, since he would be debarred from comparing his own performances with those of others. In short, our characterizations of persons and their performances as intelligent, prudent and virtuous or as stupid, hypocritical and cowardly could never have been made, so the problem of providing a special causal hypothesis to serve as the basis of such diagnoses would never have arisen. The question, 'How do persons differ from machines?' arose just because everyone already knew how to apply mental-conduct concepts before the new causal hypothesis was introduced. This causal hypothesis could not therefore be the source of the criteria used in those applications. Nor, of course, has the causal hypothesis in any degree improved our handling of those criteria. We still distinguish good from bad arithmetic, politic from impolitic conduct and fertile from infertile imaginations in the ways in which Descartes himself distinguished them before and after he speculated how the applicability of these criteria was compatible with the principle of mechanical causation.

He had mistaken the logic of his problem. Instead of asking by what criteria intelligent behaviour is actually distinguished from non-intelligent behaviour, he asked 'Given that the principle of mechanical causation does not tell us the difference, what other causal principle will tell it us?' He realized that the problem was not one of mechanics and assumed that it must therefore be one of some counterpart to mechanics. Not unnaturally psychology is often cast for just this role.

When two terms belong to the same category, it is proper to construct conjunctive propositions embodying them. Thus a purchaser may say that he bought a left-hand glove and a right-hand glove, but not that he bought a left-hand glove, a right-hand glove, and a pair of gloves. 'She came home in a flood of tears and a sedan-chair' is a well-known joke based on the absurdity of conjoining terms of different types. It would have been equally ridiculous to construct the disjunction. 'She came home either in a flood of tears or else in a sedan-chair'. Now the dogma of the Ghost in the Machine does just this. It maintains that there exist both bodies and minds; that there occur physical processes and mental processes; that there are mechanical causes or corporeal movements and mental causes or corporeal movements. I shall argue that these and other analogous conjunctions are absurd; but, it must be noticed, the argument will not show that either of the illegitimately conjoined propositions is absurd in itself. I am not, for example, denying that there occur mental processes. Doing long division is a mental process and so is making a joke. But I am saying that the phrase 'there occur mental processes' does not mean the same sort of thing as 'there occur physical processes', and, therefore, that it makes no sense to conjoin or disjoin the two.

If my argument is successful, there will follow some interesting consequences. First, the hallowed contrast between Mind and Matter will be dissipated, but dissipated not by either of the equally hallowed absorptions of Mind by Matter or of Matter by Mind, but in quite a different way. For the seeming contrast of the two will be shown to be as illegitimate as would be the contrast of 'she came home in a flood of tears' and 'she came home in a sedan-chair'. The belief that there is a polar opposition between Mind and Matter is the belief that they are terms of the same logical type.

It will also follow that both Idealism and Materialism are answers to an improper question. The 'reduction' of the material world to mental states and processes, as well as the 'reduction' of mental states and processes to physical states and processes, presupposes the legitimacy of the disjunction 'Either there exist minds or there exist bodies (but not both)'. It would be like saying, 'Either she bought a left-hand and right-hand glove or she bought a pair of gloves (but not both)'.

It is perfectly proper to say, in one logical tone of voice, that there exist minds, and to say, in another logical tone of voice, that there exist bodies. But these expressions do not indicate two different species of existence, for 'existence' is not a generic word like 'coloured' or 'sexed'. They indicate two different senses of 'exist', somewhat as 'rising' has different senses in 'the tide is rising', 'hopes are rising', and 'the average age of death is rising'. A man would be thought to be making a poor joke who said that three things are now rising, namely the tide, hopes and the average age of death. It would be just as good or bad a joke to say that there exist prime numbers and Wednesdays and public opinions and navies; or that there exist both minds and bodies. In the succeeding chapters I try to prove that the official theory does rest on a batch of category-mistakes by showing that logically absurd corollaries follow from it. The exhibition of these absurdities will have the constructive effect of bringing out part of the correct logic of mental-conduct concepts.

4 Historical note

It would not be true to say that the official theory derives solely from Descartes' theories, or even from a more widespread anxiety about the implications of seventeenth-century mechanics. Scholastic and Reformation theology had schooled the intellects of the scientists as well as of the laymen, philosophers and clerics of that age. Stoic-Augustinian theories of the will were embedded in the Calvinist doctrines of sin and grace; Platonic and Aristotelian theories of the intellect shaped the orthodox doctrines of the immortality of the soul. Descartes was reformulating already prevalent theological doctrines of the soul in the new syntax of Galileo. The theologian's privacy of conscience became the philosopher's privacy of consciousness, and what had been the bogy of Predestination reappeared as the bogy of Determinism.

It would also not be true to say that the two-worlds myth did no theoretical good. Myths often do a lot of theoretical good, while they are still new. One benefit bestowed by the para-mechanical myth was that it partly superannuated the then prevalent para-political myth. Minds and their Faculties had previously been described by analogies with political superiors and political subordinates. The idioms used were those of ruling, obeying, collaborating and rebelling. They survived and still survive in many ethical and some epistemological discussions. As, in physics, the new myth of occult Forces was a scientific improvement on the old myth of Final Causes, so, in anthropological and psychological theory, the new myth of hidden operations, impulses and agencies was an improvement on the old myth of dictations, deferences and disobediences.

READING 3

The Nature of Mind

D.M. Armstrong

Source: Armstrong, D.M. (1981) *The Nature of Mind*, Brighton, The Harvester Press, pp.1–15. First published 1980, University of Queensland Press.

Men have minds, that is to say, they perceive, they have sensations, emotions, beliefs, thoughts, purposes and desires. What is it to have a mind? What is it to perceive, to feel emotion, to hold a belief or to have a purpose? Many contemporary philosophers think that the best clue we have to the nature of mind is furnished by the discoveries and hypotheses of modern science concerning the nature of man.

What does modern science have to say about the nature of man? There are, of course, all sorts of disagreements and divergences in the views of individual scientists. But I think it is true to say that one view is steadily gaining ground, so that it bids fair to become established scientific doctrine. This is the view that we can give a complete account of man in *purely physico-chemical terms*. This view has received a tremendous impetus in recent decades from the new subject of molecular biology, a subject that promises to unravel the physical and chemical mechanisms that lie at the basis of life. Before that time, it received great encouragement from pioneering work in neurophysiology pointing to the likelihood of a purely electro-chemical account of the working of the brain. I think it is fair to say that those scientists who still reject the physico-chemical account of man do so primarily for philosophical, or moral or religious reasons, and only secondarily, and half-heartedly, for reasons of scientific detail. This is not to say that in the future new evidence and new problems may not come to light that will force science to reconsider the physico-chemical view of man. But at present the drift of scientific thought is clearly set towards the physico-chemical hypothesis. And we have nothing better to go on than the present.

For me, then, and for many philosophers who think like me, the moral is clear. We must try to work out an account of the nature of mind which is compatible with the view that man is nothing but a physcio-chemical mechanism.

And in this paper, I shall be concerned to do just this; to sketch (in barest outline) what may be called a Materialist or Physicalist account of the mind.

The authority of science

But before doing this, I should like to go back and consider a criticism of my position that must inevitably occur to some. What reason have I, it may be asked, for taking my stand on science? Even granting that I am right about what is the currently dominant scientific view of man, why should we concede science a special authority to decide questions about the nature of man? What of the authority of philosophy, of religion, of morality, or even of literature and art? Why do I set the authority of science above all these? Why this 'scientism'?

It seems to me that the answer to this question is very simple. If we consider the search for truth, in all its fields, we find that it is only in science that men versed in their subject can, after investigation that is more or less prolonged, and which may in some cases extend beyond a single human lifetime, reach substantial agreement about what is the case. It is only as a result of scientific investigation that we ever seem to reach an intellectual consensus about controversial matters.

In the Epistle Dedicatory to *De Corpore*, Hobbes wrote of William Harvey, the discoverer of the circulation of the blood, that he was: 'the only man I know, that conquering envy, hath established a new doctrine in his life-time'.

Before Copernicus, Galileo and Harvey, Hobbes remarks: 'there was nothing certain in natural philosophy'. And we might add, with the exception of mathematics, there was nothing certain in any other learned discipline.

These remarks of Hobbes are incredibly revealing. They show us what a watershed in the intellectual history of the human race the seventeenth century was. Before that time, enquiry proceeded, as it were, in the dark. Man could not hope to see their doctrine *established*, that is to say, accepted by the vast majority of those properly versed in the subject under discussion. There was no intellectual consensus. Since that time, it has become a commonplace to see new doctrines, sometimes of the most far-reaching kind, established to the satisfaction of the learned, often within the lifetime of their first proponents. Science has provided us with a method of deciding disputed questions. This is not to say, of course, that the consensus of those who are learned and competent in a subject cannot be mistaken. Of course such a consensus can be mistaken. Sometimes it has been mistaken. But, granting fallibility, what better authority have we than such a consensus?

Now this is of the utmost importance. For in philosophy, in religion, in such disciplines a literary criticism, in moral questions in so far as they are thought to be matters of truth and falsity, there has been a notable failure to achieve an intellectual consensus about disputed questions among the learned. Must we not then attach a peculiar authority to the discipline that can achieve a consensus? And if it present us with a certain vision of the nature of man, is this not a powerful reason for accepting that vision?

I will not take up here the deeper question *why* it is that the methods of science have enabled us to achieve an intellectual consensus about so many disputed matters. That question, I think, could receive no brief or uncontroversial answer. I am resting my argument on the simple fact that, as a result of scientific investigation, such a consensus has been achieved.

I may be replied – it often is replied – that while science is all very well in its own sphere – the sphere of they physical, perhaps – there are matters of fact on which it is not competent to pronounce. And among such matters, it may be claimed, is the question: what is the whole nature of man? But I cannot see that this reply has much force. Science has provided us with an island of truths, or, perhaps one should say, a raft of truths, to bear us up on the sea of our disputatious ignorance. There may have to be revisions and refinements, new results may set old findings in a new perspective, but what science has given us will not be altogether superseded. Must we not therefore appeal to these relative certainties for guidance when we come to consider uncertainties elsewhere? Perhaps science cannot help us to decide whether or not there is a God, whether or not human beings have immortal souls, or whether or not the will is free. But if science cannot assist us, what can? I conclude that it is the scientific vision of man, and not the philosophical or religious or artistic or moral vision of man, that it the best clue we have to the nature of man. And it is rational to argue from the best evidence we have.[1]

Defining the mental

Having in this way attempted to justify my procedure, I turn back to my subject: the attempt to work out an account of mind, or, if you prefer, of mental process, within the framework of the physico-chemical, or, as we may call it, the Materialist view of man.

Now there is one account of mental process that is at once attractive to any philosopher sympathetic to a Materialist view of man: this is Behaviourism. Formulated originally by a psychologist, J.B. Watson, it attracted widespread interest and considerable support from scientifically oriented philosophers. Traditional philosophy had tended to think of the mind as a rather mysterious inward arena that lay behind, and was responsible for, the outward or physical behaviour of our bodies. Descartes thought of this inner arena as a *spiritual substance*, and it was this conception of the mind as spiritual object that Gilbert Ryle attacked, apparently in the interest of Behaviourism, in his important book *The Concept Mind* (1949). He ridiculed the Cartesian view as the dogma of 'the ghost in the machine'. The mind was not something behind the behaviour of the body, it was simply part of that physical behaviour. My anger with you is not some modification of a spiritual substance that somehow brings about aggressive behaviour; rather it is the aggressive behaviour itself; my addressing strong words to you, striking you, turning my back on you, and so on. Thought is not an inner process that lies behind, and brings about, the words I speak and write: it is my speaking and writing. The mind is not an inner arena, it is outward act.

It is clear that such a view of mind fits in very well with a completely Materialistic or Physicalist view of man. If there is no need to draw a distinction between mental processes and their expression in physical behaviour, but if instead the mental processes are identified with their so-called 'expressions', then the existence of mind stands in no conflict with the view that man is nothing but a physico-chemical mechanism.

However, the version of Behaviourism that I have just sketched is a very crude version, and its crudity lays it open to obvious objections. One obvious difficulty is that it is our common experience that there can be mental processes going on although there is no behaviour occurring that could possibly be treated as expressions of those processes. A man may be angry, but give no bodily sign; he may think, but say or do nothing at all.

In my view, the most plausible attempt to refine Behaviourism with a view to meeting this objection was made by introducing the notion of a *disposition to behave*. (Dispositions to behave play a particularly important part in Ryle's account of the mind.) Let us consider the general notion of disposition first. Brittleness is a disposition, a disposition possessed by materials like glass. Brittle materials are those that, when subjected to relatively small forces, break or shatter easily. But breaking and shattering easily is not brittleness, rather it is the *manifestation* of brittleness. Brittleness itself is the tendency or liability of the material to break or shatter easily. A piece of glass may never shatter or break throughout its whole history, but it is still the case that it is brittle: it is liable to shatter or break if dropped quite a small way or hit quite lightly. Now a disposition to *behave* is simple a tendency or liability of a person to behave in a certain way under certain circumstance. The brittleness of glass is a disposition that the glass retains throughout its history, but clearly there also could be dispositions that come and go. The dispositions to behave that are of interest to the Behaviourist are, for the most part, of this temporary character.

Now how did Ryle and others use the notion of a disposition to behave to meet the obvious objection to Behaviourism that there can be mental process going on although the subject is engaging in no relevant behaviour? The strategy was to argue that in such cases, although the subject was not behaving in any relevant way, he or she was *disposed* to behave in some relevant way. The glass does not shatter, but it is still brittle. The man does not behave, but he does have a disposition to behave. We can say he thinks although he does not speak or act because at that time he was disposed to speak or act in a certain way. *If* he had been asked, perhaps, he would have spoken or acted. We can say he is angry although he does not behave angrily, because he is disposed so to behave. *If* only one more word had been addressed to him, he would have burst out. And so on. In this way it was hoped that Behaviourism could be squared with the obvious facts.

It is very important to see just how these thinkers conceived of dispositions. I quote from Ryle:

> To possess a dispositional property *is not to be in a particular state, or to undergo a particular change*; it is to be bound or liable to be in a particular state, or to undergo a particular change, when a particular condition is realized.[2]

So to explain the breaking of a lightly struck glass on a particular occasion by saying it was brittle is, on this view of dispositions, simply to say that the glass broke because it is the sort of thing that regularly breaks when quite lightly struck. The breaking was the normal behaviour, or not abnormal behaviours, of such a thing. The brittleness is not to be conceived of as a *cause* for the breakage, or even, more vaguely, a *factor* in bringing about the breaking. Brittleness is just the fact that things of that sort break easily.

But although in this way the Behaviourists did something to deal with the objection that mental processes can occur in the absence of behaviour, it seems clear, now that the shouting and the dust have died, that they did not do enough. When I think, but my thoughts do not issue in any action, it seems as obvious as anything is obvious that there is something actually going on in me that constitutes my thought. It is not simply that I would speak or act if some conditions that are unfulfilled were to be fulfilled. Something is currently going on, in the strongest and most literal sense of 'going on', and this something is my thought. Rylean Behaviourism denies this, and so it is unsatisfactory as a theory of mind. Yet I know of no version of Behaviourism that is more satisfactory. The moral for those of us who wish to take a purely physicalistic view of man is that we must look for some other account of the nature of mind and of mental processes.

But perhaps we need not grieve too deeply about the failure of Behaviourism to produce a satisfactory theory of mind. Behaviourism is a profoundly unnatural account of mental processes. If somebody speaks and acts in certain ways, it is natural to speak of this speech and action as the *expression* of his thought. It is not at all natural to speak of his speech and action as identical with his thought. We naturally think of the thought as something quite distinct from the speech and action that, under suitable circumstances, brings the speech and action about. Thoughts are not to be identified with behaviour, we think; they lie behind behaviour. A man's behaviour constitutes the *reason* we have for attributing certain mental processes to him, but the behaviour cannot be identified with the mental processes.

This suggests a very interesting line of thought about the mind. Behaviourism is certainly wrong, but perhaps it is not altogether wrong. Perhaps the Behaviourists are wrong in identifying the mind and mental occurrences with behaviour, but perhaps they are right in thinking that our notion of a mind and of individual mental states is *logically tied to behaviour*. For perhaps what we mean by a mental state is some state of the person that, under suitable circumstances, brings about a certain range of behaviour. Perhaps mind can be defined not as behaviour, but rather as the inner cause of certain behaviour.

Thought is not speech under suitable circumstances; rather it is something within the person that, in suitable circumstances, brings about speech. And, in fact, I believe that this is the true account, or, at any rate, a true first account, of what we mean by a mental state.

How does this line of thought link up with a purely Physicalist view of man? The position is that while it does not make such a Physicalist view inevitable, it does make it *possible*. It does not entail, but it is compatible with, a purely Physicalist view of man. For if our notion of the mind and of mental states is nothing but that of a cause within the person of certain ranges of behaviour, than it become a scientific question, and not a question of logical analysis, what in fact the intrinsic nature of that cause is. The cause might be, as Descartes thought it was, a spiritual substance working through the pineal gland to produce the complex bodily behaviour of which men are capable. It might be breath, or specially smooth and mobile atoms dispersed throughout the body; it might be many other things. But in fact the verdict of modern science seems to be that the sole cause of mind-betokening behaviour in man and the higher animals is the physico–chemical workings of the central nervous system. And so, assuming we have correctly characterized our concept of a mental state as nothing but the cause of certain sorts of behaviour, then we can identify these mental states with purely physical states of the central nervous system.

At this point we may stop and go back to the Behaviourist's dispositions. We saw that, according to him, the brittleness of glass or, to take another example, the elasticity of rubber, is not a state of the glass or the rubber, but is simply the fact that things of that sort behave in the way they do. But now let us consider how a scientist would think about brittleness or elasticity. Faced with the phenomenon of breakage under relatively small impacts, or the phenomenon of stretching when a force is applied followed by contraction when the force is removed, he will assume that there is some current state of the glass or the rubber that is responsible for the characteristic behaviour of samples of these two materials. At the beginning, he will not know what this state is, but he will endeavour to find out, and he may succeed in finding out. And when he has found out, he will very likely make remarks of this sort: 'We have discovered that the brittleness of glass is in fact a certain sort of pattern in the molecules of the glass'. That is to say, he will *identify* brittleness with the state of the glass that is responsible for the liability of the glass to break. For him, a disposition of an object is a state of the object. What makes the state a state of brittleness is the fact that it gives rise to the characteristic manifestations of brittleness. But the disposition itself is distinct from its manifestations: it is the state of the glass that gives rise to these manifestations in suitable circumstances.

This way of looking at dispositions is very different from that of Ryle and the Behaviourists. The great difference is this: If we treat dispositions as actual states, as I have suggested that scientists do, even if states the intrinsic nature of which may yet have to be discovered, then we can say that dispositions are actual *causes*, or causal factors, which, in suitable circumstances, actually bring about those happenings that are the manifestations of the disposition. A certain molecular constitution of glass that constitutes its brittleness is actually *responsible* for the fact that, when the glass is struck, it breaks.

Now I cannot argue the matter here, because the detail of the argument is technical and difficult, but I believe that the view of dispositions as states, which is the view that is natural to science, is the correct one.[3] I believe it can be shown quite strictly that, to the extent that we admit the notion of dispositions at all, we are committed to the view that they are actual *states* of the object that has the disposition. I may add that I think that the same holds for the closely connected notions of capacities and powers. Here I will simply have to assume this step in my argument.

But perhaps it will be seen that the rejection of the idea that mind is simply a certain range of man's behaviour in favour of the view that mind is rather the inner *cause* of that range of man's behaviour, is bound up with the rejection of the Rylean view of dispositions in favour of one that treats dispositions as states of objects and so as having actual causal power. The Behaviourists were wrong to identify the mind with behaviour. They were not so far off the mark when they tried to deal with cases where mental happenings occur in the absence of behaviour by saying that these are dispositions to behave. But in order to reach a correct view, I am suggesting, they would have to conceive of these dispositions as actual *states* of the person who has the disposition, states that have actual causal power to bring about behaviour in suitable circumstances. But to do this is to abandon the central inspiration of Behaviourism: that in talking about the mind we do not have to go behind outward behaviour to inner states.

And so two separate but interlocking lines of thought have pushed me in the same direction. The first line of thought is that is goes profoundly against the grain to think of the mind as behaviour. The mind is, rather, that which stands behind and brings about our complex behaviour. The second line of thought is that the Behaviourist's dispositions, properly conceived, are really states that underlie behaviour and, under suitable circumstances, bring about behaviour. Putting these two together, we reach the conception of a mental state as *a state of the person apt for producing certain rangers of behaviour.* This formula: a mental state is a state of the person apt for producing certain ranges of behaviour, I believe to be a very illuminating way of looking at the concept of a mental state. I have found it fruitful in the search for detailed logical analyses of the individual mental concepts.

I do not think that Hegel's Dialectic has much to tell us about the nature of reality. But I think that human thought often moves in a dialectical way, from thesis to antithesis and then to the synthesis. Perhaps thought about the mind is a case in point. I have already said that classical philosophy has tended to think of the mind as an inner arena of some sort. This we may call the Thesis. Behaviourism moves to the opposite extreme: the mind is seen as outward behaviour. This is the Antithesis. My proposed Synthesis is that the mind is properly conceived as an inner principle, but a principle that is identified in terms of the outward behaviour it is apt for bringing about. This way of looking at the mind and mental states does not itself entail a Materialist or Physicalist view of man, for nothing is said in this analysis about the intrinsic nature of these mental states. But if we have, as I have argued that we do have, general scientific grounds for thinking that man is nothing but a physical mechanism, we can go on to argue that the mental states are in fact nothing but physical states of the central nervous system.

[...]

As I have emphasized before, I have done no more than sketch a programme for a philosophy of mind. There are all sorts of expansions and eludications to be made, and all sorts of doubts and difficulties to be stated and overcome. But I hope I have done enough to show that a purely Physicalist theory of the mind is an exciting and plausible intellectual option.

Notes

1 The view of science presented here has been challenged in recent years by new Irrationalist philosophies of science. See, in particular, Thomas Kuhn (1962) and Paul Feyerabend (1975). A complete treatment of the problem would involve answering their contentions.

2 Ryle, 1949: 43; emphasis added.

3 I develop the argument in *Belief, Truth and Knowledge* (1973), Ch.2, sect. 2.

References

ARMSTRONG, D.M. (1973) *Belief, Truth and Knowledge*, Cambridge, Cambridge University Press.

FEYERABEND, P. (1975) *Against Method*, London, New Left Books.

KUHN, T. (1962) *The Structure of Scientific Revolutions*, Chicago, University of Chicago Press.

RYLE, G. (1949) *The Concept of Mind*, London, Hutchinson.

Index